Wild country camping

# Wild country camping

Kevin Walker

Constable London

First published in Great Britain 1989
by Constable and Company Limited
10 Orange Street London WC2H 7EG
Copyright © 1989 by Kevin Walker
Set in Linotron Times 9 pt by
Rowland Phototypesetting Limited
Bury St Edmunds, Suffolk
Printed in Great Britain by
The Bath Press Limited
Bath, Avon

British Library CIP data
Walker, Kevin
Wild country camping
1. Camping. Manuals
I. Title
796.54

ISBN 0 09 468930 X

To Guy and Paul

# Contents

# Illustrations

*Photographs by Kevin Walker*

# Diagrams

# Acknowledgements

This book could not have been written without the help of many people. In particular I would like to thank John, Jeff and Sarah at Crickhowell Adventure Gear for their time, their expert advice on equipment and the endless cups of coffee. Choosing the right gear at the right price would be so much easier if all shops were like this! John deserves special mention for scribbling a variety of comments (not all of them rude) on the first draft.

I would also like to thank T. J. P. Davenport, LLB, for his patient help in explaining the legal position to someone who gets totally confused by law books. The credit for accuracy is his; the fault for any inaccuracy, mine.

My thanks, too, go to all those people with whom I have camped in the wilds and from whom I have learnt so much. Many started as acquaintances and became, almost overnight, lifelong friends.

Last, but by no means least, I must acknowledge the 'assistance' given by my eighteen-month-old daughter, Kelly Megan, who delights in pushing various buttons on the word processor at the most inconvenient of times!

# Foreword

One of my earliest experiences of wild country camping was an unmitigated disaster! It happened one Easter when a friend and I decided to spend a few days in Snowdonia before returning to college. Having scrounged a lift with an early-morning lorry driver, we arrived in Capel Curig at about eight o'clock on a grey and blustery morning.

Being poor students, we were sleeping rough, and had with us a cheap 'mountain tent' (at least that's the way it was described on the label!) and various other pieces of supposedly essential camping equipment. Split between the two of us, the weight didn't seem too bad, but by the time we had added our food, spare clothing, the various odds and ends we thought we would need, plus a fairly comprehensive assortment of rock-climbing gear, we were staggering around like two lame tortoises.

We had both listened to the weather forecast the previous night and, although it was not good, we saw little cause for concern. Shouldering our packs, we set off up Moel Siabod with no definite plans other than reaching Tremadoc Cliffs by the following afternoon, where we had agreed to meet up with some friends from the college climbing club. Being interested in what can best be described as 'mountain heritage', we were hoping to spend a few hours poking around the old slate mines and associated buildings which lie around the head of Cwm Orthin, and this seemed to be as good a spot as any to make camp for the night. The next day we could easily drop down to Croesor and, if the weather was fine, could even enjoy a quick jaunt up Cnict and still get down to Tremadoc in time for a couple of climbs.

Having made an early start, we thought we had plenty of time, so wandered along at a very easy pace. However, the weight of our packs became more and more oppressive as we climbed, and we made heavy weather of the ridge. After a long rest on the summit, we headed downhill towards Clogwyn Bwlch-y-maen before sweating up on to Y Cribau – a short ascent which we punctuated with frequent stops to gaze at Llynnau Diwaunedd through wisps of hill fog.

The wind began to strengthen as we plodded up Cerrig Cochion and on to Moel Meirch, and what with battling against the gusts and humping vast quantities of largely useless gear, we were starting to feel very tired by the time we had dropped down to Llyn Edno and climbed on to Ysgafell Wen. After another very welcome rest near Llynnau'r Cwn, we staggered on towards the summit of Moel Druman, then down the ridge towards the head of Cwm Orthin.

By the time we reached Llyn Clogwyn brith we had had enough! The visibility was down to less than 20 metres, the wind was threatening to blow us off our feet and the now torrential rain was making life generally unpleasant. Although the old mines were less than a kilometre away, the lake was fairly sheltered, and we decided to pitch camp.

It was now that our troubles really began. We had never used the tent before and had problems pitching it – mainly because the poles didn't want to fit together. We also found that there were insufficient pegs. By the time we had jury-rigged the thing and crawled inside, the surrounding area had become a quagmire and it was as wet and muddy inside the tent as it was outside! Our fumbling fingers found lighting the stove well nigh impossible and we constantly brushed against the walls of the tent as we moved around trying desperately to find some semblance of comfort. Within an hour the tent material started to display all the properties of a large mesh net.

Luckily our sleeping bags were of reasonably good quality, bought in the light of experience after some fairly horrendous nights spent in Scottish bothies the previous winter. Filled with man-made fibre, they retained a fair amount of their insulating properties even when wet, but by about midnight we realized that our situation was getting silly. Despite the sleeping bags, we were cold, wet, tired and thoroughly miserable. The tent was next to useless (indeed by this time we were lying in about 10 centimetres of water), our stove had gone on strike, and we saw little point in putting on our dry clothing because it would immediately have become wet. We came to the conclusion that anything was better than this, so packed up our stove and sleeping bags, donned our boots and waterproofs, and battled our way down to the mine, leaving the tent until the following day.

I will never forget that journey. Cold, stiff muscles refused to work; the mountain appeared malevolent, tripping us at every opportunity; our head-torches seemed to give little if any light. It was a bruised, battered and thoroughly depressed pair who eventually reached the chill haven of Rhosydd No. 7 Adit. Having visited this mine before, we knew that there was a small, dank chamber only a short way inside, and on reaching this we stripped off and put on dry clothes, wrung as much water as we could from our sleeping bags, lined them with our survival bags, and crawled inside. The stove burst into life on the first attempt and we passed the rest of the night in relative luxury!

The following morning we emerged like two damp troglodytes to find that the storm had blown itself out. Patches of blue sky appeared from between ragged shards of stratus and, having squelched up to collect the saturated remains of the tent, we staggered down to Croesor carrying the extra weight of several gallons of water, a sadder but wiser pair. The tent found its final resting place in a litter-bin on the side of the road between Croesor and Tremadoc, and we vowed never again to camp in wild country.

However, the hills have always called me with an irresistible magnetism and it was less than six weeks before I found myself again inside a tent on the side of a mountain. This time the weather was kind and the experience memorable. Further trips inevitably followed, and by the next time I was caught in bad weather I had managed to collect some reasonable gear and, arguably more important, had sorted out a routine. Despite two horrendously inclement nights, I managed to keep warm, dry and comfortable, and had a far more enjoyable time than would have been the case had I returned to a valley base each evening.

I am now an enthusiastic wilderness-camper and gain a tremendous amount of satisfaction and enjoyment simply from spending a few days in the middle of nowhere. I've spent numerous pleasant nights huddled amongst the boulders of rocky ridges, in the middle of the vast nothingness of windswept moors, beside mirror-still mountain pools, even in echoing chambers underground. I cannot, in all honesty, pretend that every camp has been luxurious, but in the vast majority of cases these experiences have been happy ones, and I have returned to the real world feeling refreshed and revitalized.

In this book I have tried to distil what I consider to be the basics of the camping experience. Like all other aspects of mountain activities, wild country camping is essentially a very personal adventure, and the things I like will not necessarily be the things you like (and vice versa). As long as I persuade some of you that living in wild country need not be uncomfortable and give those already converted a little food for thought, I will be well satisfied.

Kevin Walker
Llangynidr
November, 1988

# Introduction

There can be little doubt that more and more people are taking to the mountains and moorlands in order to get away from it all. Many return to civilization each night to enjoy the comfort of bed and breakfast, whilst others pitch their tents in more or less formal valley camp sites where a variety of facilities, however basic, are reasonably close to hand.

That being said, increasing numbers of outdoor enthusiasts are finding that both their enjoyment of the surroundings and their sense of relaxation and adventure can be increased dramatically when they forsake civilization for several days at a time, their nights being spent in the wilds, living 'rough'. I emphasize the word rough because many people associate camping with discomfort, especially camping in the middle of nowhere. However, with the application of a little 'campcraft' – that strange and indefinable mixture of technique, skill and experience – it is possible for all of us to rough it in comfort!

In the context of this book, 'wild country' can be described as the type of terrain found, for example, in any of the ten National Parks, in mid-Wales and throughout Scotland – anywhere, in fact, where the nearest habitation is at least two hours away, even in good conditions. Further details of areas you might like to visit can be found in Appendix I.

It must be emphasized that this is not a book about 'mountaincraft'. Throughout this volume I have made the assumption that the reader is already an enthusiastic hill-walker and has, at the very least, a basic knowledge of mountain safety, map and compass techniques, etc. If this is not the case, can I draw your attention to Appendix IV, where you will find a number of suggestions for further reading, and in particular to my two previous books – *Mountain Navigation Techniques* and *Mountain Hazards* (both published by Constable) – which in many ways form companion volumes to this book.

A basic knowledge of mountaincraft should be regarded as being of the utmost importance. Make no bones about it, like many other forms of mountain activities, camping in wild country can, at worst, be uncomfortable, frustrating, gruelling and even downright dangerous. However, it need not be this way, particularly when combined with good mountaincraft. Indeed, when the routine works and everything falls almost miraculously into place, it can be a magical and very tangible experience, full of a primitive reality which seems to increase the further one is from habitation. Dawn and dusk take on a significance and beauty far greater than that which we generally afford them, and on crisp, clear nights there is little that beats lying on one's back, staring at a profusion of twinkling stars, watching satellites and meteorite showers. Conversely, as anyone who has been in the situation will tell you, riding out a mountain storm from the isolation of a remote camp site can be an extremely humbling experience. One thing is certain, whatever the conditions: you can guarantee that you will see, hear and feel things, the memory of which will remain with you for the rest of your life.

In order to try and make some sense out of a welter of information, I have divided this book into three main parts. The first deals with equipment in all its many and varied forms, describing tents and shelters, sleeping bags, cooking equipment and utensils, and various bits and pieces which some may see as essential and others may be happy to do without. Obviously one has to carry all this gear, and Part One of the book ends with a discussion on the large-capacity rucksacks.

I have tried, wherever possible, to describe the equipment in its basic forms, discussing the whys and wherefores rather than looking at specific models. In this way I have tried to ensure that the book will not be out of date before it is published! One of the problems facing the novice is that there is such a wide range of equipment available, it is often difficult to decide which is the most suitable for any given job. I hope the decision will be that much easier after reading the relevant sections.

In any event, I thoroughly recommend that you visit a reputable specialist mountaineering equipment retailer before buying anything. Ask to see a range of models and discuss the pros and cons of each before you commit yourself. Good equipment is not cheap and mistakes can be costly. Bearing this in mind, it is not a bad idea to ask the sales assistants what equipment they use and why. If you find they are not enthusiasts themselves, I suggest that you are in the wrong shop, for it is impossible to give good advice about this type of equipment unless you have personal experience of it, and of the types of conditions under which it will be used. For similar reasons it is unwise to buy equipment via mail order unless, of course, you have had previous experience of it.

In Part Two we are concerned more with the camping experience itself, and there are discussions on planning and preparation, food and drink requirements and how they can best be met, choosing suitable sites, and camp routine. Some people may not like the sound of having a routine – after all, most people visit wild areas to get away from such things – but there is no doubt that some form of routine can make all the difference between pain and pleasure, especially in inclement weather conditions. There is also a brief discussion of some of the extra factors which should be borne in mind during extended trips in remote areas.

The final part of the book gives a few suggestions for areas which you might like to visit, plus a brief discussion of the position of the law with regard to where you can and cannot legally camp. After all, wherever you are in Britain, however wild and remote the area, someone owns the land. I also make mention of the Country and Mountain Codes, suggest sources for further reading and list several addresses which you may find useful.

**Part One**

# Equipment

## 1.1 Introduction

One of my most memorable times on the hill was spent in the north-west highlands of Scotland in September. More by luck than by judgement, our timing was perfect, and we enjoyed a week of superlative weather. Indeed, conditions were so good, the nights so warm and calm, that for three consecutive nights we slept on beds of heather beneath the stars, leaving our sleeping bags and tents still packed in our rucksacks. Whilst this was an experience that I can highly recommend, conditions are not usually so kind, and generally speaking you should be prepared to cope with inclement weather.

In this part of the book we will be looking in detail at the different types of equipment available, concentrating more on the basic requirements and design features of each type rather than simply giving a description of specific models. As with general walking and climbing gear, there is a wealth of choice from a growing number of manufacturers, and this can seem confusing not only to first-time buyers but to the more experienced user as well. Advances in materials and construction techniques are being made all the time and a piece of equipment that was once regarded as being the top of the range can quickly be relegated to second place by a new development. It is therefore vitally important that you understand why a particular piece of equipment is designed in a certain way, and also that you recognize the inherent advantages and shortcomings of the various designs.

However, as discussed in Part Two, even if you possess the very best camping equipment there is no guarantee that you will have a comfortable time. As in mountain navigation, when the possession of a map and compass is only the first stage in finding your way around, it is of little use carrying all this gear unless you know how to use it. It is therefore vitally important that you get to know your equipment before you use it in earnest. In this respect I can only hope to point the way to successful trips – the rest is up to you.

The experience I related in the Foreword could have been totally avoided with a little foresight. We should have practised putting the tent up before we took it into the hills; we should have been able to light our stove in any conditions. At the risk of repeating myself, you must get to know your gear before you use it in the wilds. Pitch your tent in the back garden or on a valley site before taking it up into the mountains. If you come across any problems, try to rectify them before you set off for real. However, it is only of limited use getting to know your tent on a warm, windless day, for the probability is that the first time you use it in the hills it will be blowing a gale. Try pitching it on a blustery day or in a rainstorm and see what a difference it makes! Similarly, cook a couple of meals on your stove before you disappear into the back end of nowhere. Again, don't just practise in good conditions; the next time you use it you could be cold and tired, hunched up against torrential rain and a howling, bitter wind.

Finally, as I said in the Introduction, I have assumed that you are already a more or less competent mountain visitor and, as such, that you know something of the types of equipment and clothing which you should have with you whenever you visit the hills. It therefore goes without saying that you have a comfortable pair of walking or climbing boots, know something about the Layer System with regard to clothing, and recognize the few really essential items which should always be in your pack. If this is not the case, you would be well advised to get these essentials first, leaving the more adventurous camping trips until you are better equipped to enjoy them. There is no reason, however, why you should not gain some basic camping experience at lower or less remote sites, for such experience is never wasted, and will doubtless go a long way to making your later camps more enjoyable.

## 1.2  Tents and shelters

When I first started camping in wild country, choosing a tent was not too much of a problem. There were only about ten suitable models available and most of these shared the same basic design

features. Nowadays the situation is totally different and the shops
are full of a vast range of differing models of all shapes, sizes and
materials. However, if you boil it down to basics there are
effectively only three designs: ridge tents, tunnel tents and various
types of dome tents. There are also a number of strange-looking
hybrid designs which purport to make use of the best features of
each.

BASIC FEATURES
A tent suitable for use in wild country needs to fulfil a number of
different functions. Unfortunately, many of these tend to be
mutually exclusive and this means that, in effect, there is no such
thing as the ideal tent. This is especially true if you also take
personal preferences into consideration.

In order be anywhere near efficient, your tent should possess a
number of features, no matter what the basic design. It should, for
example, be light and compact whilst still being weatherproof and
stable, and should preferably be easy to pitch, strike and pack. In
this respect, some of the modern hybrid designs can seem
mind-bogglingly complicated, and no matter what tent you
eventually choose, you should practise pitching and striking it
before you use it for real. Knowing how your tent goes up and down
can make a vast amount of difference, particularly in windy
weather, although, despite what the sales brochure may tell you,
the tent that is easy to pitch or strike in a high wind has yet to be
invented.

If it is to be at all weatherproof, your tent should be of a
double-skin construction (but see also page 28). This means that
the inner tent should be totally enclosed by a 'down-to-earth'
flysheet which covers not only the walls but also the door or doors.
Maintaining the separation between the inner tent and the flysheet
is of the utmost importance, and the inherent separation of the two
layers is far easier to maintain in some designs than in others (Fig.
1). Not only does this space provide insulation but, far more
important, it plays a large part in the weatherproofing qualities.

The basic idea in double-skin construction is very similar to that
of a cavity wall in a house. The main purpose of the flysheet is to

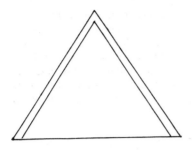

Ridge tent. Separation
difficult to maintain in side
winds unless there are well
designed side guys.

Dome tent. Good
separation.

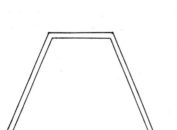

Wedge tent. Separation
difficult to maintain at roof
section and poor in side winds.

**Fig. 1. Separation in different tents.**

shed any water that falls upon it. If not made of a waterproof material there will be a certain amount of leakage, but any moisture that does get through should, in theory, run down the inside of the flysheet and therefore will not get inside the tent. However, if the separation between the flysheet and the inner tent is not maintained and the two layers of material rub together, moisture will inevitably find its way to the inside of the tent and will then run down the walls and collect on the groundsheet.

You may think that one of the obvious ways around such a problem would be to use a totally waterproof material for both the flysheet and the inner tent, but unfortunately this leads to condensation. Many of you will be familiar with the problems of condensation caused by wearing waterproofs made from non-breathable materials. Exactly the same can happen in tents. If the inner tent is constructed from a waterproof material, the moisture which we all produce in the form of invisible perspiration and in exhaled breath (plus any extra moisture produced during cooking, etc.) will condense on the walls of the inner tent, eventually running down to form pools on the groundsheet. However, if the inner tent is made from a permeable or breathable material, any such condensation will pass through the walls and condense on the inside of the flysheet where it will do little harm – assuming that the separation is maintained.

This works well under most conditions, but there are times when condensation forms on the permeable material of the inner tent as well. This normally occurs during exceptionally cold or humid weather, when wet clothing or equipment is brought inside, or when you are forced to cook inside the tent. The problem is especially noticeable if you decide to make a brew inside the tent during the early hours of a bitterly cold winter's night! Under such circumstances it is advisable to have some form of ventilation, and many tents have mesh panels which are designed to minimize the problem. However, these are not always totally effective, and an additional and very useful feature is to have double-ended zips on the door. It is then possible to open the door slightly from the top, thus creating a form of chimney effect without causing too much of a draught.

In order to prevent water, snow and draughts from entering the inner tent, the door or doors should be fitted with zips at all junctions (including along the base). There should also be a sewn-in groundsheet, the material of which extends up the walls of the inner tent for some distance (certainly not less than 10 centimetres) thus creating a form of waterproof tray. Additionally, all the materials used should be such that the whole structure is stable and robust enough to stand up to the full range of mountain or moorland weather. It is, for example, of little use if your tent rains water on to you during a downpour. Similarly, a pole which breaks during a mountain storm can lead to serious problems, and may literally become a matter of life or death.

You will obviously find it a distinct advantage if you can enter and exit from the tent without having to resort to painful or complicated contortions, and there should be sufficient internal space to enable you to live comfortably without feeling cramped. In inclement weather or when the tent is being used for long periods, such as in a base camp situation, it is advisable to have a space in which you can store wet gear, preferably beneath the flysheet but not in the inner tent. Many designs incorporate some form of 'bell-end' or provide a suitable space between a vertical inner wall and sloping flysheet. In bad conditions it is also extremely useful if you can *safely* cook in, or at least very close to, the entrance of the tent, but bear in mind the problems of condensation as outlined above, and do not forget that the vast majority of camping injuries are burns and scalds (see also Sections 1.4 and 2.5).

Although some tents are made more stable and rigid by means of a multitude of guy lines, this is something which you should try to avoid if at all possible. Not only is it aggravatingly fiddly to have yards of line which have to be secured, it also means that you have to carry more pegs (more of which anon), and such lines tend to have the infuriating habit of tripping you up with monotonous regularity, no matter how careful you are. A well designed tent should be inherently stable and will therefore need a minimum of guy lines, which may only need to be pegged out during particularly stormy weather.

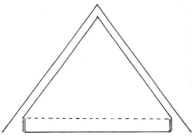

**Fig. 2. Sewn-in groundsheet.** Note how the groundsheet forms a tray. The sides extend up the walls of the inner tent and form a lip at the entrance.

MATERIALS

The most important function of your tent is to protect you from the elements. In order to do this with anything like an acceptable level of efficiency, the material from which the flysheet is made should be both waterproof and windproof. The groundsheet should be an integral part of the inner tent (i.e. sewn-in – Fig. 2), and this too should be waterproof. As it will have to put up with a fair amount of wear and tear, it also needs to be fairly durable. You are going to have to carry the tent on your back along with everything else, so all the materials used in its construction need to be light in weight and low in bulk, whilst still retaining the necessary properties of strength and durability which will enable them to cope with the severity of wilderness weather. When you take all this into consideration, it is not really surprising that, at the time of writing, there is no such thing as the perfect tent material.

Various forms of cotton fabric were, for many years, regarded as the traditional tent material, mainly because there was little else available. The big disadvantage of cotton is its weight, especially when saturated with moisture, and the lighter cotton fabrics generally do not have the necessary strength to cope with severe weather. It is still possible to buy all-cotton tents of traditional design but they tend to be heavy, starting at around 5 kilograms for the smaller one- to two-person models. There are also a number of problems associated with rot and mildew (although most modern cotton fabrics are proofed in some way). On the plus side, a good quality cotton tent can give years of service so long as it is well maintained (see also page 49).

The lighter weight cotton fabrics are still used occasionally for inner tents because they have a 'comfortable feel' and can help to reduce condensation. Although, personally, I like a cotton inner tent, it has to be said that they are still heavier than the majority of synthetic fabrics, especially if they absorb moisture, in which case they can take a fair amount of time to dry. Under certain circumstances, they also have a nasty habit of causing drips if you accidentally lean against them. For these reasons, the vast majority of modern tents are made from all-synthetic fabrics, the most common material being nylon.

Nylon fabrics are non-absorbent, relatively easy to waterproof and extremely strong. This means that a tent made from fabrics weighing as little as 1.5 grams per square metre can be as strong (if not stronger) than a similar design made from a far heavier cotton fabric. A typical modern lightweight tent will have a breathable nylon inner tent, a proofed nylon flysheet (sometimes made of ultra-lightweight rip-stop material), and a heavier weight, proofed nylon groundsheet. Proofing is normally done with polyurethane (pu) or acrylic coatings, although heavier and more durable groundsheets proofed with neoprene or PVC are also available, and are often fitted as standard on the larger tents. One further point worth noting is that any untaped seams on the flysheet or groundsheet should be coated with a proprietory seam sealant.

One disadvantage of these materials is that they can make an incredible amount of noise, even in a light breeze. Certain fabrics crackle like sweet-papers and can lead to sleepless nights! The biggest drawback, however, is condensation. As mentioned above, if the separation between flysheet and inner tent is maintained, this should not happen. However, with certain designs of tent (particularly those with flat roof sections), and under certain conditions, condensation can be a major problem, far more so than with tents made from cotton fabrics.

Tents made from 'breathable' waterproof fabrics (such as Goretex$^{TM}$) are also available, and these need only be single-skin. This means that they tend to be very lightweight (even though

Goretex™ is heavier than standard nylon) and they are generally
far easier to pitch than their double-skin counterparts. The
materials themselves are made in such a way that they allow water
vapour to pass through whilst keeping out water droplets.
Theoretically, they should prevent those problems associated with
condensation, and when used for clothing, Goretex™ in particular
works very well. However, when used in tents there are a number of
other factors which must be taken into consideration.

Although you do not need to know the theory of how these
fabrics work, it is important that you have a basic understanding of
the principle. In order to drive the water vapour through the fabric,
the vapour pressure on the inside has to be greater than the vapour
pressure on the outside. Put more simply, the climate inside the
waterproof shell has to be warmer and more humid than the climate
outside. In shell garments this is not too much of a problem, but in
the larger spaces to be found in tents, the internal vapour pressure
may not be high enough to allow the fabric to work, and the vapour
may therefore condense on the tent walls. For this reason there is an
optimum size for tents made of these fabrics, and most of the
effective models are very small. They also tend to work better if the
ventilation is poor!

Even in these small tents, and particularly during extended use in
extremely humid conditions, the brushed inner surface of the fabric
may become so saturated with condensed vapour that moisture
starts to run down the taped seams, forming pools on the
groundsheet. In these conditions you can also get wet simply by
brushing against the fabric.

It is perhaps worth noting that, because the British climate is
fairly humid, such tents tend not to work too well. They are far
better suited to expedition use in drier climates, be they either hot
or cold.

CONSTRUCTION METHODS
If you buy a tent made by one of the better-known mountaineering
equipment manufacturers, there should be few problems associated
with the method of construction. However, a few guidelines will not
go amiss.

**Fig. 3. Lap-felled seam.** Note how the two layers of fabric are brought together and wrapped around each other before being sewn.

The strongest seams are those constructed by the flat, lap-felled method, in which the fabric edges are folded around each other before being sewn together (Fig. 3). Seams in waterproof materials, such as those used in the flysheet and groundsheet, should either be coated with seam sealer, or hot-taped by the manufacturer. Seams in breathable waterproof materials must be hot-taped.

Stitching varies considerably in quality, and it is worth checking it before you buy your tent. A lock stitch is infinitely better than a chain stitch (which will run if a fault develops), and the stitches should be evenly spaced and uniformly tensioned, running straight along the entire length of the seam. Crooked stitching, uneven tension and badly lapped seams are all potential areas of weakness. Up to a point, the more stitches there are, the better – there certainly should be no fewer than 3 to 4 stitches per centimetre.

The most awkward places to sew are areas such as tight corners and the ends of zips, and it is worth checking these places carefully. If the stitching is good here, it will most likely be good throughout. However, it is a good idea to check generally for bad finishing and loose ends where the stitching stops, and for small areas of uncaught fabric.

The quality of the stitching can be crucial in areas such as apexes, the end of pole sleeves, the junction of seams and at peg loops. Peg loops in particular should be bar-tacked or reinforced in some other way in order to give extra strength.

TENT POLES

The type of pole you have will depend very much upon the design of the tent. The more traditional ridge tents and their modern equivalents should have hollow poles made from a lightweight aluminium alloy. The separate sections of each pole are often linked

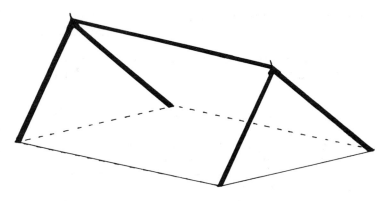

**Fig. 4. Standard A-frame ridge tent.**

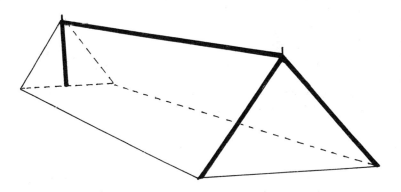

**Fig. 5. Sloping ridge tent.**

together with either an elastic shock-cord or a form of spring arrangement, although nesting or telescopic poles are available for some models.

The strongest (and heaviest) ridge tents usually employ 'A' poles at either end, the larger models often having a ridge pole as well. This makes for a very stable structure around which the tent is pitched (Fig. 4). Typically such tents are all cotton and are designed primarily for 'base camp' use, or for other situations where strength is a more important consideration than weight. To save weight, some models have single upright poles at each end, but this also results in a reduction in both stability and ease of access.

Smaller, sloping ridge models are also available, in which the ridge slopes from an 'A' pole at the front down to a single, short 'upright' pole at the back (Fig. 5). Here again, the 'A' poles may be replaced by a single upright and the ridge pole may be absent, although this will result in similar reductions in stability and convenience.

A variation on the sloping ridge tent theme is the wedge, in which the 'A' pole at the front is replaced by two uprights. Whilst this gives a better space-to-weight ratio, the design is nowhere near so stable, and the flat roof section can cause problems by trapping rain and snow, and may result in condensation dripping on to the inner tent.

Most modern designs of tent employ fairly thin, flexible poles made of either hollow aluminium alloy, or hollow or solid fibreglass. Alloy poles are generally regarded as being the best, and the sections of each pole are usually linked together by elastic shock-cord to make threading them through the pole sleeves slightly easier. One disadvantage is that they are prone to kinking unless you take great care of them.

Lightweight fibreglass poles are generally weaker than those made from alloy, and the heavier and cheaper varieties are often used in 'budget' tents. They are reasonably efficient but have a reputation for shattering and the ends are prone to splitting. However, new composite materials are being developed all the time, and you should not take the presence of fibreglass poles to mean that the tent is not of the best quality. I cannot

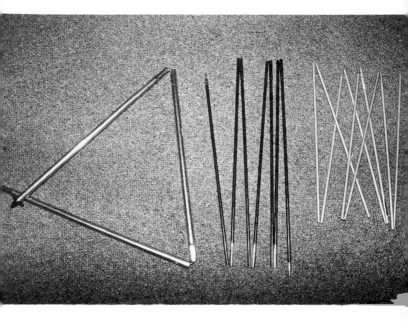

A selection of modern tent poles. From left to right: standard alloy, flexible alloy, and solid fibreglass.

over-emphasize how important it is to visit a reputable mountaineering equipment retailer before buying any gear.

Further details of some of the different designs of tents available will be found starting on page 36.

TENT PEGS
Do not make the mistake of underestimating the importance of tent pegs! Whatever its design, even if it is supposedly self-supporting, a tent must be efficiently anchored to the ground if it is to be at all effective. A common error is to think that the pegs supplied with the tent are the best available. Sadly, this is rarely the case. Indeed,

many manufacturers simply bung in a load of cheap (often heavy) pegs, just to show willing.

There are many different types of peg available; some have been designed for specific ground conditions, others are too heavy or cumbersome to be ideal for use in wild country. The standard peg tends to be the alloy (or heavier steel) skewer which is available in several lengths, the 18 centimetre and 23 centimetre versions being the most popular. The better quality skewers are good, all-round pegs which can be used in most situations. However, they tend to cut through sandy soils, bend in stony ground, and slither about uncontrollably in muddy conditions. Although they will soon cut through unconsolidated snow, if the area around them is compacted they will often freeze-in, giving excellent support.

Angle or curved pegs are available in a variety of lengths in both steel and alloy, and these tend to hold more successfully in muddy or sandy soils. They also freeze-in well in compacted snow. There are chunky plastic pegs which are good in muddy and peaty conditions (although the 'hooks' on the top have a habit of breaking in some models), weird-looking screw-in pegs for hard or stony ground, and a whole welter of other designs. Also available are 'storm anchors' (Fig. 6) which effectively double-up the peg points

**Fig. 6. Storm anchor.**

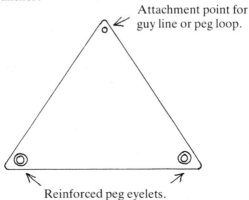

Attachment point for guy line or peg loop.

Reinforced peg eyelets.

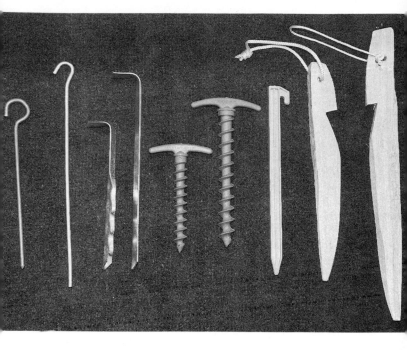

A selection of tent pegs. From left to right: 18 cm and 23 cm skewers, short and long angles, short and long screw-in plastic, short and long wood.

for storm guys, etc. An acquaintance of mine never goes camping without taking two 'traditional' wooden pegs which he swears will hold when all else pulls out!

Skewers are ideal to form the bulk of the pegs you carry with you, although most people like to take a small number of angles or plastic pegs, and it may be prudent to include a couple of screw-in pegs if you are visiting a particularly hard or rocky area. Despite the fact that weight is an important consideration, it is probably better to have too many pegs than too few, and you would be well advised to carry some spares.

TENT DESIGNS

It is the area of tent design that most people find confusing, for there are a multitude of tents available in a wealth of shapes and sizes. I have already mentioned that there is no such thing as the ideal tent: all designs tend to have inherent advantages and disadvantages, and some designs are more suitable for particular applications than others.

Make no mistake about it, a good tent is not going to be cheap. As with most other forms of outdoor gear, you generally get what you pay for, and it is probably best to spend as much as you can afford. The 'mountain tent' used on the trip mentioned in the Foreword cost us just under £40 and lasted one night – not the most economical way to do it! It would have been far more sensible if we had slept in barns or bunkhouses and saved our money until we could have afforded something better.

Most people will not be able to afford a tent for every application, so it makes sense to go for a good, all-round model. It is important to realize that just because a tent is expensive and is described as a 'mountain tent', it does not necessarily mean that it is suitable for the British mountains. There are, for example, some excellent and very expensive mountain tents designed for use in extremely dry, cold conditions which are totally unsuitable for the wet and windy weather which is generally experienced in Western Europe. Assuming that you have taken note of the basic design features which should be included in a tent, the vast majority of mistakes are caused by inappropriate choice of model rather than bad design or construction. Hopefully the following descriptions should go some way towards making the choice that much easier.

*Standard ridge tents* (Fig. 7)

For many years, ridge tents were the firm favourites for wild country camping, although they are now losing a little ground to some of the more modern designs. The heavy duty models usually have an 'A' pole at each end, often supporting a horizontal ridge pole, and a rectangular sleeping area (although some models have a triangular extension to the rear, usually described as a 'bell-end'). Specialist versions for expedition use are available, and these may

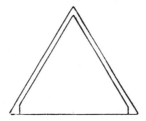

**Fig. 7. Example of a standard ridge tent.**

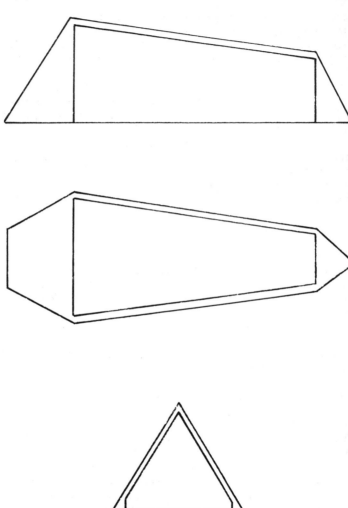

**Fig. 8. Example of a sloping ridge tent.**

have snow valances (extra panels of material around the base on which snow can be piled), special vents to try and reduce condensation, and a wealth of guy lines for extra stability. Normally designed to accommodate two or three people, the standard models tend to be fairly simple, reasonably durable and exceptionally stable in severe weather, and this makes them suitable for high-level, year-round use. On the negative side, they are expensive and heavy (typically between about 5 and 8 kilograms), although this weight can be shared between two people.

Lighter weight models are available. In these, the 'A' poles are replaced with uprights, and the ridge pole may be absent. This leads to a reduction in stability and ease of access, and such models are not really suitable for four-season, high-level use. Whatever the pole arrangement, the triangular cross-section means the living space is somewhat constricted, and gear storage and bad-weather cooking is not particularly convenient.

*Sloping ridge tents* (Fig. 8)
Basically a modification of the standard ridge design, these tents have an 'A' pole (or single upright) at the front, from which the ridge slopes down to a short, single pole at the rear. There may or may not be a ridge pole. Designed to accommodate one or two people in a tapering sleeping area, they typically weigh between 2 and 4 kilograms, and are generally relatively cheap and simple. The versions with ridge and 'A' poles are suitable for three-season, high-level use, but the stability of those with uprights and no ridge pole is not so good, especially in high winds. The living area is very constricted, as is cooking and storage space.

*Transverse ridge tents* (Fig. 9)
These represent a further modification of the standard ridge design in which the rectangular sleeping area lies across, as opposed to along, the ridge, resulting in a slightly larger living area (two to three people) and greater storage/cooking space. The structure is usually supported by two uprights and a ridge pole, which does not make it the most stable of designs. Unsuitable for use at high levels, they are nevertheless simple and reasonably light and compact (typically between 2 and 4 kilograms).

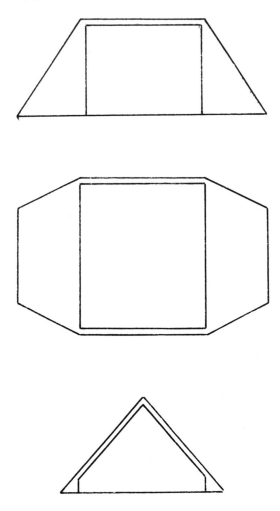

**Fig. 9. Example of a transverse ridge tent.**

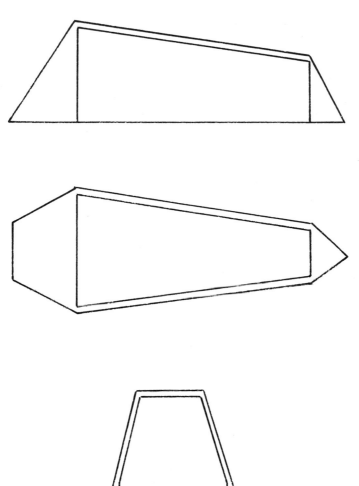

**Fig. 10. Example of a wedge tent.**

*Wedge tents* (Fig. 10)
These form yet another modification of the ridge design in which
the front end has been squared off to give greater space and ease of
access. Support is usually by two uprights at the front, and one
shorter upright at the back. Although space is enhanced by the
steeper side walls, giving enough space for up to two people in a
tapering floor area, the structure is not particularly stable and is
unsuitable for high-level use. Additionally, although reasonably
light and cheap, such designs require careful pitching in order to
maintain the separation between the flysheet and the inner tent.
Some flat roof designs can also cause problems by trapping snow
and water, and allowing condensation to build up until it drips on to
the inner tent.

We now move on to the more modern designs, in which rigid
poles have been replaced by thin flexible poles of fibreglass or alloy.
In general, these all give a better space-to-weight ratio having a
semicircular as opposed to triangular cross-section.

*Single hoop tents* (Fig. 11)
In this design a single flexible pole is used to support an arch over a
rectangular sleeping area large enough for one or two people.
Although this gives a useful internal volume, storage and cooking
space is usually limited; however transverse designs are available.
Since they are relatively light (from about 1.5 kilograms upwards),
simple and fairly stable, they make ideal single-person tents suitable
for four-season use, and single-skin versions made from breathable
fabrics are available. However, certain models do not cope well in
side winds.

*Tunnel tents* (Fig. 12)
There are many different types of tunnel tent available, varying
from double-hooped versions with tapering accommodation, to
triple-hooped versions with rectangular or coffin-shaped sleeping
areas suitable for three persons. They are generally reasonably light
(from about 2 kilograms upwards), relatively easy to pitch
(particularly the two pole models) and competitively priced.

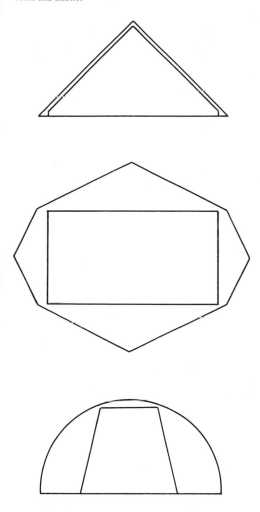

**Fig. 11. Example of a single hoop tent.**

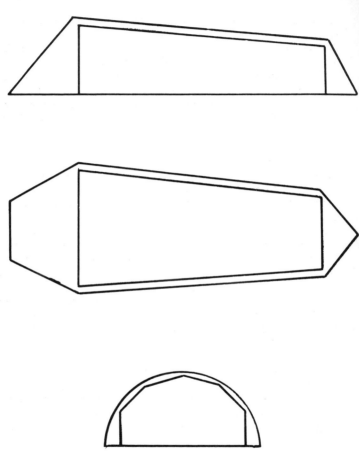

**Fig. 12. Example of a tunnel tent.**

Although they tend to make the most use of the available space, storage and cooking areas can be limited in some designs. Additionally, most models tend not to like high winds or snowfall, and are therefore unsuitable for high-level or four-season use.

Tunnel tents with reinforced ridges are also available. These can give greater storage and cooking space and are generally more stable than the standard designs, but they are naturally heavier and more expensive, somewhat more complicated to pitch, and still do not function very well in side winds.

*Crossover dome tents* (Fig. 13)

There are a number of different crossover designs available, most using either two or three flexible poles bent to form a simple dome. In the simplest designs, the poles all cross at the apex; in more advanced versions the crossover point is offset slightly to give greater stability. They tend to be expensive and fairly heavy (typically around 4 to 5 kilograms) but provide a lot of usable space (two to four people) in either hexagonal or rectangular sleeping areas (some have porch extensions), are relatively easy to pitch, and are becoming very popular. Offset designs are suitable for high-level, four-season use. Simple crossover designs are less stable and have been known to 'implode' in high winds. Check that the seams are sealed across the apex.

*Geodesic dome tents* (Fig. 14)

Geodesic dome tents make use of a number of flexible hoops (often four, sometimes more) linked together to form a complicated patchwork of panels in an attempt to create a stable structure which makes the greatest use of the available space. Whilst there is little doubt that these are roomy tents, the stability of some models is not all that it could be, although most designs are suitable for four-season, high-level use. With enough space to accommodate from three to six people, they tend to be on the heavy side (from 4 to more than 7 kilograms), and are very expensive. They can also be extremely complicated to pitch.

Also available are modified geodesic domes which try to make use of the best features of tunnels, crossover domes and full

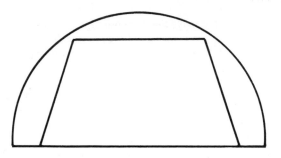

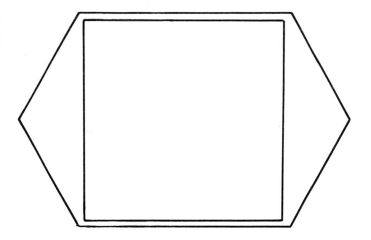

**Fig. 13. Example of a crossover dome tent.**

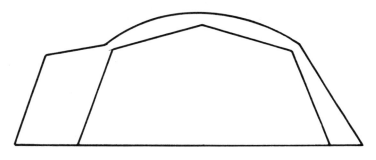

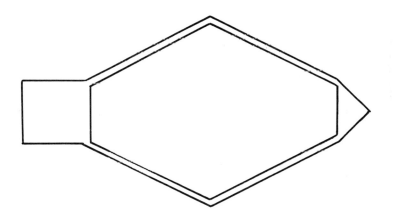

**Fig. 14. Example of a geodesic dome tent.**

geodesics. These usually have a rectangular sleeping area which will accommodate from two to four people, are often lighter (from 3 to 5 kilograms) and are far cheaper. Generally more stable than crossover dome designs and giving a useful amount of usable space, certain models may be regarded as attractive propositions suitable for high-level, four-season use.

CHOOSING A TENT

Assuming that you are spending a fair amount of money, any mistake you make is going to be costly, so it pays to get it right first time. Not only that, if you use a tent in weather conditions or situations for which it was not designed, you can run the risk of all sorts of difficulties. Hopefully the preceding pages will have given you some idea of what to look for and what to avoid. Before parting with any money, however, you would be wise to ask yourself a number of questions.

*How much room will you want?* There are a number of factors to be considered here. Will you, for example, be camping alone (either solo or with others but in your own tent) or will you be sharing? If sharing, how friendly are you with your companion? Are you a tidy individual or do you, like me, tend to spread?

If you are intending to camp in winter, you will generally need more space than in summer when much of your time may well be spent outside the tent. Cooking in cramped conditions inside the tent during a snowstorm, surrounded by wet clothing and odd bits of gear, is not going to do much for your mental health! Generally speaking, a one-man tent is exceptionally small, and many people prefer a small two-man tent for solo use. Don't just go by the description: ask to see the tent when pitched (better still, put it up yourself and see how easy or not it is to pitch), and think about how you would feel spending a day in it, perched on the side of a mountain in stormy conditions.

*Will you be using the tent as a base from which to explore the surrounding area or for brief overnight stops?* If staying in one spot for more than a couple of days, you will probably want more space than if you are constantly on the move, striking camp early and pitching elsewhere later on. In the same way, you should also consider such things as ease of access in inclement conditions (can you remove wet gear under cover without saturating the inner tent?), cooking in similar conditions (will you have to cook inside the tent or is there space under the flysheet?), and gear storage (do your wet waterproofs and muddy boots live in the tent with you?).

*When will you be using the tent?* A tent which is ideal for summer use may be totally the wrong choice if you intend to camp during winter. For high-level winter camping you are going to need a sturdy tent, possibly either a geodesic dome or a standard ridge design with 'A' poles. Generally speaking, if you intend to camp regularly in wild country in winter you would be well advised to buy a tent with a four-season rating.

*How durable is the groundsheet?* Many lightweight tents have groundsheets made from a fairly flimsy coated material which can easily puncture. Additionally, the coating itself can wear away leading to leakage. If you choose this type of tent it may be worth your while buying some thin, closed-cell foam material to place between the groundsheet and the ground (see also page 66).

One further point worth noting is the modern controversy which rages about the relative merits of inner- or flysheet-first pitching. In my opinion, the argument has got totally out of hand and it really doesn't matter which way your tent goes up so long as it is well designed and constructed. Exponents of inner-first pitching will tell you that it results in a more stable structure and ensures that the tent is pitched tautly, thus helping the all-important separation between the flysheet and inner tent. Conversely, flysheet-first fans say the big advantage is that you can erect the inner under cover without running the risk of getting it wet, and because the guys are attached more or less directly to the poles, the structure is far stronger. A number of tent designs allow them to be pitched either way and, needless to say, I honestly don't believe it makes a significant difference one way or the other.

AFTERCARE
Once you have splashed out vast amounts of money on a tent, you will obviously want it to last for as long as possible. The golden rule is never to store the tent wet for any length of time. Even though

modern synthetic fabrics do not rot, damp storage is not going to do the tent much good.

After every trip, clean off any dirty marks, remove any pieces of grit, mud and vegetation which may be stuck to the groundsheet, and give the whole tent a good airing before rolling it up for storage. Cleanliness is definitely next to Godliness when it comes to looking after a tent! At the same time, check that everything is complete: make sure you have sufficient pegs, that all the poles and any connectors are there, and that guy lines are serviceable, untangled, and securely attached. If peg attachment points are in the form of rubber rings, it is worth checking these regularly as they are prone to perishing. Any faults such as small tears, scuffs or loose stitches should be attended to; some manufacturers produce repair kits (at extra cost, of course) for just this eventuality. Major faults such as torn panels or split seams may have to be repaired by the manufacturer, many of whom have excellent after-sales service.

Always bear in mind that the next time you use your tent you might be caught in a storm, so it is in your own interest to make sure that it is kept in good condition.

ALTERNATIVE FORMS OF SHELTER

In most cases you will be glad to pitch your tent and get inside, but if you visit the wilds with any sort of regularity there are bound to be occasions when the weather conditions and surroundings make it almost sacrilegious to house yourself in a cocoon of nylon or cotton. If you are lucky enough to meet such conditions, do not feel you have to pitch your tent just because you carried it with you; a night spent in the open can be a memorable experience. Do not forget, however, that the weather can change with remarkable speed. If conditions deteriorate to the extent that you need to use your tent, you will find it much easier if it is already pitched. Starting to make camp in deteriorating conditions in the early hours of the morning may well become a memorable experience, but the memories will not be all that pleasant!

Occasionally the weather may be so mild that you can simply sleep as you are, but if you are fairly high in the mountains you will generally find that it starts to get cold in the early hours, and most people will like to have a sleeping bag to hand. With or without a sleeping bag, you will probably be amazed at the amount of cold and dampness which rises from the ground and you will undoubtedly find it warmer if you lie on some form of insulation. This usually takes the form of a sleepmat (see page 65).

Any breeze will also have a noticeable chilling effect as the night progresses, and you may need to construct some form of windbreak. It may be possible to do this simply by making use of the local topography (i.e. lying beside a boulder) but there will be times when you will need to resort to Heath-Robinson affairs constructed from survival bags or flysheets supported on tent poles or such like. However, if – as suggested above – you have already pitched your tent, you are not going to be able to use your tent poles! The solution to this problem is limited solely by your imagination.

Similar considerations apply on a sultry night when there is a possibility of drizzle. You could, of course, burrow into a survival bag, but this is not a particularly comfortable experience due to the amount of condensation that will form. Indeed, if you are also inside a sleeping bag, using a survival bag in this way will simply make your sleeping bag damp and this could lead to problems on succeeding nights, especially if you intend to camp for any length of time. In this type of situation, it is far better to use your tent or construct some other form of shelter.

I do not believe it would be advantageous to describe any particular form of shelter as what you construct will depend very much upon the conditions, the local topography and the materials which you have available. Again, really the only limiting factor is your imagination. Emergency shelters for use during accidental benightment or in emergency situations are beyond the scope of this book. If you wish to know more about these, basic details can be found in my previous book, *Mountain Hazards* and in some of the other books mentioned in Appendix IV.

BIVOUAC BAGS
One final piece of equipment that may be of interest is the bivouac bag, more commonly known as a 'bivi' bag. In its most basic form this is simply a rectangular sack made from a totally waterproof and

The bivouac bag. Room for you and your sleeping bag, but little else!

windproof, breathable material (Goretex$^{TM}$ being the most common and, at the time of writing, probably the most efficient), entry to which is gained by a zip or press studs, usually covered with a baffle which is held in place by velcro. Baffled zips are by far the most effective. Various models and styles are available, from those with bases made of groundsheet material (cheaper and more durable but less effective) to those in which one or more flexible hoops can be inserted to make the bag reminiscent of a small tunnel tent.

While these are undoubtedly less comfortable and convenient than a tent, they are very effective and are comparatively small and light. They are not cheap, however, and most people will prefer to pay a little more and get a reasonable quality tent.

Usage is about as basic as one can get: you simply get inside your sleeping bag inside your bivi bag and that's it. There's little, if any, room to store gear, and cooking in inclement conditions can be a nightmare. They are not suitable for high-level, four-season use for any length of time, although those hardened individuals who really want to rough it may find them a tempting proposition.

## 1.3  Sleeping

If a good quality mountain tent is important, so too is a suitable sleeping bag. Even if conditions are such that you can sleep outside the tent, nights which are warm enough to allow you to go without a sleeping bag of some form or another tend to be few and far between – especially if you are half-way up a mountain.

When it comes to choosing their first sleeping bag, many people are bewildered by the wide range of types, styles and fillings available. Furthermore, certain descriptions can be confusing: what exactly, for example, is a 'five-season rating'? Luckily, however, if you boil it down to basics, choosing a suitable sleeping bag should not be too much of a problem. As with tents, it will be helpful to look at the basic theory behind sleeping bag construction and to find out how they work.

In its simplest form, a sleeping bag is constructed of two bags of fabric, one inside the other, and the space in between is filled with some kind of insulating material, the main purpose of which is to trap air (Fig. 15). It should be fairly obvious that a sleeping bag does not heat up of its own accord; what it does is trap air which has been warmed up by the heat of the body. In other words, it simply prevents heat loss. There are a number of different types of filling and these are discussed in more detail below.

In addition to trapping air and preventing heat loss, the insulating material and bag fabric must allow water vapour to escape. The average adult produces a surprisingly large amount of fluid each

Most specialist shops carry a large range of sleeping bags with different designs and fillings.

night and this obviously has to be dispersed somehow.

The insulating material must be held in place or it would move about between the two bags, leading to a lack of insulation in some areas and thus resulting in 'cold spots'. Certain insulating materials are more prone to movement than others, and therefore a suitable form of construction for one type of material may be totally inappropriate for another. The various types of construction will be discussed later.

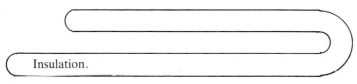

Insulation.

The main purpose of the insulation is to trap air.

**Fig. 15. Simple sleeping bag.**

TYPES OF FILLING
The cheapest sleeping bags are filled with kapok. As cheap 'starter' bags for summer use they are OK but they are not really suitable for wild country. Sleeping bags filled with Terylene are usually warmer but in practice they are not much better, for to be at all efficient they will be both heavy and bulky.

For our purposes, the main choice is between fillings of synthetic materials (usually constructed of some form of polyester fibres) and fillings of natural materials such as down and down/feather mixes. Each has inherent advantages and disadvantages.

*Synthetic-filled bags*
There are a number of different types of synthetic-filled sleeping bags available, the most suitable making use of some form of polyester fibre. The cheaper versions usually contain hollow fibre or Hollofil™ but versions containing a slightly more advanced form of filling such as 3D Hollofil™ and Quallofil™ are available. Although these latter fillings are usually only found in the more expensive sleeping bags, they have the advantage of being (warmth-for-warmth) less bulky and somewhat lighter.

The filling itself (whatever its type) can take two forms. In some bags the polyester fibres are formed into layers held together with resin. These layers are known as 'batts'. In lightweight sleeping bags of this type there is often only one layer, but this may result in cold spots. A more common approach is to use two layers which are offset to one another in a warmer but heavier bag.

The main advantage of using batts is that the filling is very stable and tends not to move around (or migrate). However, the resin results in a slight increase in weight, and the insulation of the material may be reduced because it cannot expand (thus trapping more air) beyond limits controlled by the nearest line of stitches.

The other form of synthetic filling is that in which the bag is blown-filled with loose fibres. In this case the method of construction of the sleeping bag itself is of the utmost importance, as bad or inappropriate design can lead to the filling moving about causing cold spots. Generally speaking, synthetic-filled sleeping bags are heavier and bulkier than their natural-filled counterparts, although in the more expensive bags the difference can be negligible. To put this comparison into perspective, it is probably best to say that a good quality synthetic sleeping bag is *almost* as warm, *slightly* more bulky, but *much* cheaper than a similar weight natural-filled model.

Apart from the price difference, the big advantage of the synthetic fillings is that they retain much of their insulating properties when wet. Natural fillings, on the other hand, become next to useless if they get wet, the feathers or down clumping together in a soggy mess which can take days, even weeks, to dry out.

Bearing all this in mind, it is hardly surprising that many people tend to choose a synthetic-filled sleeping bag for their first purchase.

*Natural-filled bags*
When people talk about natural-filled bags they usually refer to them as 'down-filled'. However, there is more than one type of natural filling, and some are far more effective than others.

The *crème de la crème* of natural fillings is *eiderdown*. This is incredibly warm, light and low in bulk. However, real eiderdown is in scant supply, being virtually unobtainable since the 1940s for a variety of reasons. If you are lucky enough to have a sleeping bag (or duvet) filled with pure eiderdown, hang on to it as it is a superb investment! It is unlikely that you will find such a sleeping bag in your local gear shop and even less likely that you will be able to afford it if you do!

The best type of down currently available (but only to those with large bank balances) is *goosedown*. In the better quality sleeping bags of this type the filling will be about 95% pure goosedown, the rest comprising small, curled feathers which cannot be separated from the main bulk of the material.

*Duckdown* is more commonly available than either of the previous two and this is what will be found in most 'pure down' sleeping bags. At best, it is only marginally inferior to goosedown but it can vary quite considerably in quality. New down is obviously best but occasionally it will be mixed with recycled down, resulting in a bag which is cheaper but also somewhat inferior.

*Down/feather* mixes are available from a number of manufacturers and the quality depends on the percentage of down used. At the top of the range such mixes will contain about 50% duckdown, but you would be well advised to enquire more deeply about the rest of the filling as the quality of the feathers used can vary significantly. With such mixed fillings, the insulation qualities are obviously inferior to that of pure down and the weight can also be increased to a surprisingly noticeable extent.

Down is undoubtedly the best insulation material for use in sleeping bags. Weight-for-weight it is warmer, lighter and less bulky than any synthetic material currently available and it also transmits water vapour far better. Sleeping bags of this type are, however, expensive and must be kept dry if they are to be at all effective.

SLEEPING BAG CONSTRUCTION
The way a sleeping bag is put together is equally as important as its filling, if not more so. If the sleeping bag simply consisted of two sacks of material, one inside the other, any filling would be free to move about between the two layers and this would inevitably result in a variable thickness (and, therefore, a variable degree) of insulation. In order to overcome this, manufacturers have resorted to a number of solutions, some more effective than others. Additionally, different types of filling require different construction methods.

Whatever the type of insulation material, the easiest way to stop the filling from moving about is to use a form of simple quilting (Fig. 16). However, this is not very effective because it leads to cold spots

Potential cold spots along all the seams.

**Fig. 16. Simple quilting.**

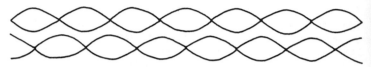

**Fig. 17. Double quilting.**

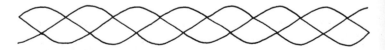

**Fig. 18. Box wall construction.**

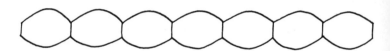

**Fig. 19. Overlapping tube construction.**

**Fig. 20. Slant wall construction.**

along the lines of stitches. Double-quilting (Fig. 17), in which the filling is separated into two quilted layers and the lines of stitches offset, is a good solution, although the extra layer/s of fabric needed result in a considerable increase in weight.

The standard way of overcoming the problem with natural or blown synthetic fillings is to use a box wall construction (Fig. 18). In this method the filling is isolated in small boxes, effectively restricting its movement. So long as each box is well filled and the walls are not too shallow, the result is a sleeping bag with no cold spots. A similar design (used predominantly with natural fillings) is the overlapping tube construction (Fig. 19). Although this is a highly efficient method, it tends to be both heavy and expensive.

Slant wall construction (Fig. 20) is very efficient, and results in a sleeping bag which is warmer (but more expensive) than any of the methods described so far. The sleeping bag will also be somewhat heavier due both to the extra fabric used and the extra filling needed.

Box and slant wall constructions are often used with blown synthetic fillings and some manufacturers include some form of 'radiant barrier' (a thin layer of heat-reflecting material) which, in theory, could increase the effective insulation by up to 20%. In practice, most manufacturers use the radiant barrier to reduce the weight and bulk of the sleeping bag whilst maintaining a high level of performance.

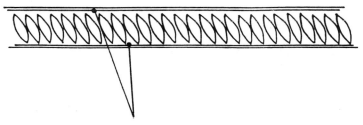

Extra thin batts along the top and base.

**Fig. 21. Sandwiched batts.**

Finally, in some high-performance synthetic-filled sleeping bags, batts of insulation are sandwiched between the inner and outer fabrics, the insulation sometimes being increased by further thin batts against the fabric shells (Fig. 21). This results in extremely efficient thermal insulation but again it increases the weight of the sleeping bag quite considerably.

OTHER DESIGN FEATURES

There are a number of other factors worth bearing in mind when choosing a sleeping bag. The quality of the shell material plays an important part in the life of the sleeping bag, particularly with natural or blown synthetic fillings. The fabric must be woven in such a way that it does not allow any of the filling to escape and should be fairly durable, resistant to rot, reasonably light in weight and low in bulk. It should also be permeable in order to transmit water vapour. Nylon fabrics would seem to fit the bill perfectly but for those people who cannot stand the feel of nylon against the skin, certain sleeping bags are available with cotton (or polycotton) inners. Although many will find such bags more comfortable, using such materials results in a sleeping bag which is slightly heavier and more bulky than a similar model constructed only of nylon fabrics.

The stitching also has an important part to play. If poor stitching leads to the collapse of any of the baffles, the thermal efficiency of the sleeping bag will be reduced. As with tents, it is advisable to check the quality of the stitching before you buy. There should be a minimum of 3 to 4 stitches per centimetre (preferably more), seams and quilting lines should be straight and even, and there should be no loose stitches or run backs at the end of any quilting lines.

Whether you choose a sleeping bag with or without zips is mainly a matter of personal preference. Short zips can be very useful for ease of entry while full-length, two-way zips can help with ventilation on a warm night. If you camp with a partner who has a similar sleeping bag, full-length zips can also aid friendship (assuming the zips are on opposite sides of the sleeping bag!). However, they do lead to an increase in weight (however marginal) and there is nothing more frustrating than crashing out for the night only to find that the zip has jammed or broken. An uncovered zip also represents a cold spot, so you should check that there is a baffle of insulated fabric which completely covers the zip for its entire length.

Size and shape, again, are largely a matter of personal preference, but there are certain factors which should be considered. If a sleeping bag is too large, its thermal efficiency will be reduced because you have to warm up extra air. On the other hand, if it is too small, you are going to feel cramped and uncomfortable, and bear in mind that you may well want to sleep in it fully-clothed in particularly cold conditions. Generally speaking, you should be able to do it up around the shoulders (or do up the hood) without your feet touching the end.

Sleeping bags are usually rectangular, tapering, coffin-shaped or mummy-shaped (Fig. 22). The latter two shapes have the advantage that they prevent excessive heat loss from around the shoulders. An integral hood or some form of shoulder baffle can also make a large difference in this respect. Bearing this in mind, you should find a shape in which you feel comfortable. Don't be shy – try the sleeping bag out on the shop floor! Try turning over in it – does it turn with you or do you turn in it? Not that it really matters either way, but it is important that you feel comfortable. Try to imagine spending a night in it half-way up a mountain in stormy conditions.

The shape of the foot end of the sleeping bag is important too. If the upper and lower parts of the bag are simply sewn together there will inevitably be a cold spot along the seam and the feet will feel constricted. One way around this is to have a fish-tail foot (Fig. 23) which gives more space, although a box-foot construction (Fig. 24) is not only comfortable but also much warmer.

SLEEPING BAG RATING

The warmth or effective insulation of sleeping bags is usually quoted in 'seasons'. These ratings – for our purposes – go from two-season to (somewhat confusingly) five-season! A two-season rating means that the sleeping bag is suitable for use in late spring, summer and early autumn. A three-season rating is given to a sleeping bag warm enough for spring, summer and autumn use and, depending on the quality of the filling, valley camping in winter.

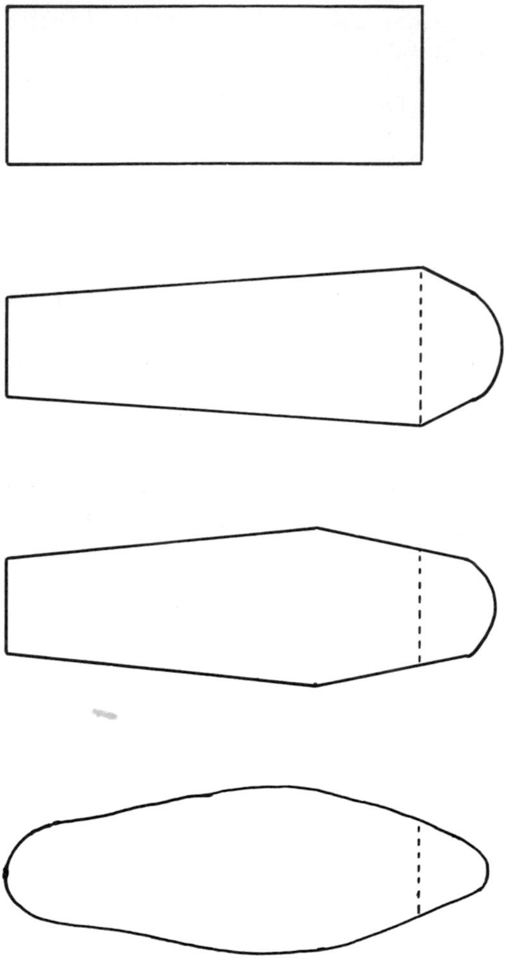

Rectangular bag without hood.

Tapering bag with hood.

Coffin-shaped bag with hood.

Mummy-shaped bag with hood.

**Fig. 22. Sleeping bag shapes.**

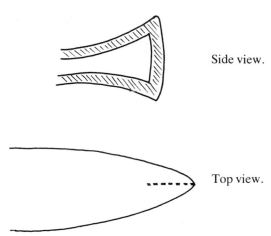

Side view.

Top view.

**Fig. 23. Fish-tail foot.** In this design the upper and lower parts of the sleeping bag are sewn together vertically giving more room for the feet.

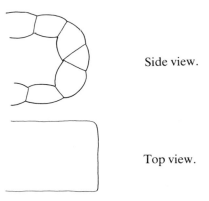

Side view.

Top view.

**Fig. 24. Box-foot.** In this design two or more extra sections are added to the foot of the sleeping bag giving plenty of room and extra insulation.

Four-season sleeping bags are for general use throughout the year and five-season ratings are reserved for those sleeping bags suitable for high-level winter use where extremely low temperatures can be expected.

Unfortunately, different manufacturers seem to have different ideas about the average temperatures that can be met during the various seasons, so it is wise to find out the lowest temperature for which the bag was designed. Do not forget, also, that people of different build can cope with different amounts of cold. Given the same temperatures, thin people may well need a bag of a higher rating than those people who are of a heavier build.

SLEEPING BAG LINERS

If you intend to camp in all seasons, you may well have difficulty in choosing a suitable sleeping bag. Some people plump for a good quality three-season sleeping bag with a full-length zip, ventilating the bag in summer, and wearing extra clothing (thermal underwear or suchlike) in winter.

Another way around the problem is to use some form of sleeping bag liner. Although you can buy cotton liners (designed to keep the inside of the sleeping bag clean more than anything else), we are more concerned with those liners made from some form of thermal material, the two most common materials being polypropylene (thermal underwear material) and fibre-pile. Both types weigh similar amounts, but those made from fibre-pile tend to be far more bulky.

These thermal liners usually have a rating of about one-season. Thus, in addition to the fact that you may be able to use the liner by itself in summer, when used in conjunction with a sleeping bag they can effectively raise the rating by a full season. Some people therefore choose a three-season sleeping bag plus a thermal liner, in this way covering almost all their options. Of the two types, fibre-pile is more luxurious (being extremely comfortable against the skin), very durable and offers good underbody insulation (see below).

The beneficial side of this method is that it is very adaptable and far cheaper than buying two sleeping bags. However, a three-season sleeping bag plus liner is heavier and more bulky than a four-season sleeping bag.

## CARE AND STORAGE

A good sleeping bag may well represent a sizeable investment and you will obviously want it to last for as long as possible. So long as you look after it properly, there is no reason why it should not last a lifetime.

The sleeping bag should be stored hanging up in a dark but airy place (the back of a wardrobe is ideal), *not* on a shelf in its stuff sack. When you come to pack it ready for your rucksack, don't fold and roll it, but literally stuff it into its stuff sack. If space is at a premium, you can use a compression sack instead of (or in conjunction with) the stuff sack. A compression sack is simply a form of stuff sack with a number of straps which can be pulled tight to compress the sleeping bag to a small size.

On arrival at your camp, take the sleeping bag from the stuff sack, shake it out, and – if possible – let it breathe and loft up before you get into it. The next morning, assuming the weather is fine, air the sleeping bag over the ridge of the tent, turning it inside out once any condensation which may have formed on the outside of the bag has disappeared.

Try to keep your sleeping bag as clean as possible. Washing a sleeping bag can be both difficult and delicate, especially with natural fillings, and requires a special soap (available from most good outdoor gear shops). It is best not to wash down bags too often as it is all too easy to affect the loft and therefore the insulation properties.

## SLEEPMATS

I said earlier that a sleeping bag keeps you warm by trapping air. Because the weight of your body compresses the insulation material between you and the ground, you will soon find that a fair amount of cold can seep upwards from underneath you. The solution is to use a sleepmat.

In its most basic form, a sleepmat is simply a rectangle of closed-cell foam which is placed between the sleeping bag and the groundsheet. These are available in different thicknesses (some have season ratings) and in various lengths (e.g. full-length or torso-length). Although predominantly designed to insulate against rising cold, they also have a slight cushioning effect on hard ground. They are also useful as 'sit-mats' during the day. Make sure the sleepmat is made of closed-cell as opposed to open-cell foam. The latter is virtually useless for our purpose and will act like a sponge if there is any moisture about.

Another possibility, usually sold off the roll, is a thinner sheet of closed-cell foam placed beneath the groundsheet. They do not insulate quite so well but do protect the groundsheet from sharp stones and general abrasion.

If you are looking for real comfort and are prepared to put up with the considerable extra weight and bulk, various forms of self-inflating mattresses are available at a price. Conversely, those of you who really want to rough it can pack the underneath of the groundsheet with heather or bracken and place spare clothing underneath the sleeping bag.


## 1.4   Cooking

Arguably the most important single piece of camping equipment you need to buy is your stove. You should be able to find (or construct) some form of shelter even if you have no tent and you should also be able to gain any necessary extra warmth from your spare clothing even if you have no sleeping bag. However, trying to cook yourself that all-important hot meal on a fire fuelled with damp grass, green heather or freshly cut peat is taking the spartan life a little too far.

An open camp fire is often regarded as a rare luxury these days, but even if you are lucky enough to be camping at a site where there is sufficient dry material available, there is a real art in cooking over glowing embers. More often than not the result of your efforts will be food which gets burnt and charred in pots which become indelibly blackened. Moreover, unless you get the fire just right whilst you are cooking, you will have to dodge either showers of painful sparks or clouds of choking, acrid smoke.

All this, however, is by way of a digression, because if you are camping in a valley site the landowner may well forbid open fires, and if you are on open moorland or mountain slopes you will probably be faced with a lack of suitable fuel. Which brings us back to the importance of stoves.

TYPES OF STOVE
As with all other items of modern gear, you will have to choose between several different types of stove. Perhaps the easiest way to make a suitable choice is to classify the stoves according to the type of fuel used and to look at the inherent advantages and disadvantages of each. Straightaway we can discount solid fuel and jelly fuel stoves. These are fine as a standby or for emergency use but are simply too inefficient to be used as your main source of heat.

*Gas stoves*
Gas is undoubtedly the most convenient and cleanest fuel available. The stoves are simple to use, the flame control is usually fairly good, and because they require no priming, they are easy to light. This latter feature, in particular, is very useful in the early hours of a winter's morning when you want to make a quick brew or warm up the tent. However, it is important that you realize that the standard cartridges contain butane which is impossible to light at temperatures of below about −1°C. Although this problem can be overcome to a certain extent by using cartridges filled with propane or a butane/propane mix (assuming, of course, they are available for your type of stove), it is safe to say that gas stoves, in general, do not like cold temperatures.

There are two main types of stove in common usage: those using resealable cartridges and those using non-resealable cartridges. Those using resealable cartridges are obviously more convenient as they can be broken down into their component parts and are therefore easier to pack and carry. Although it is possible to buy a special adaptor which clamps over certain of the non-resealable cartridges allowing them to be removed from the burner, such adaptors represent yet another piece of equipment (and therefore extra weight) to be carried.

Gas stoves. The models at either end pack away into their own set of pans.
The two right-hand models use non-resealable cartridges.

Gas stoves remain extremely popular with general campers but
they are one of the most expensive types when it comes to running
costs. Moreover, the cartridges (which are fairly bulky, even when
empty) may not be available in remote areas. They also have a
limited burning time and, no matter what the temperature, they
tend to burn at an infuriatingly slow rate once you have used up
about two-thirds of the fuel. This is particularly noticeable in cold
conditions when, as has been noted, they may be difficult or even
impossible to light. They are also extremely sensitive to draughts
and have a fairly low heat output compared with certain other
stoves.

Some models pack away very neatly, the burner itself taking up
very little space, but assembling and disassembling such stoves can
be awkward. With these models there is also the danger that you
may lose one or more of the parts, making the stove totally useless.
Also available are very compact stoves which fit inside integral
pans.

The drawback of these is that the cartridges are fairly small and therefore have a relatively limited life.

Although preferred by education authorities and youth groups for safety reasons, gas stoves are not foolproof. Changing cartridges, especially the non-resealable types, should be done outside, well away from naked flames, and it is unwise to store a stove or the spare cartridges in the tent. Both propane and butane are heavier than air and any gas that leaks will build up in a layer across the groundsheet thus leading to a danger of explosion, or even suffocation at night.

*Paraffin pressure stoves*
Paraffin-burning pressure stoves are initially fairly expensive but are extremely efficient, very economical and give a good heat output. Together with petrol pressure stoves they are probably the most commonly used form of heating in wild country camping. The fuel is readily available in most areas and will seldom ignite if accidentally spilled, and the stove itself offers a high degree of flame control which is unaffected by the ambient temperature. Indeed, in cold conditions you can sit the stove directly on snow without there being an appreciable decrease in efficiency. In terms of durability, such a stove will last a lifetime if looked after correctly.

There are, however, several disadvantages on top of the high initial cost, the main one being that such stoves require priming. Not only does this mean you have to carry either methylated spirits or some form of priming paste with you, but priming itself can be a tricky process until you get to know your stove. Pumping (or pressurizing) the stove too early can result in a dangerous 'flare' which could be disastrous if conditions have forced you to cook inside the tent. If you do accidentally spill any fuel or if any fuel leaks from its container, not only will it take ages to evaporate but it will also make everything in its vicinity stink for days afterwards.

Finally, all pressure stoves tend to be on the heavy side, and although the heat output can be phenomenal, they tend to be sensitive to draughts.

*Petrol pressure stoves*
Petrol pressure stoves are identical to those burning paraffin in a
number of respects. They are, for example, extremely efficient and
economical, very durable and certain models have a stupendous
heat output. Unfortunately, they are also fairly heavy, sensitive to
draughts and the initial cost is high. That being said, it is possible to
buy certain models which consist purely of a burner and fuel line
with an integral pump which screws into the top of a standard fuel
container. Such stoves are obviously far lighter and less bulky than
the more traditional models.

Most petrol stoves require priming but this can be done with
petrol, thus making it unnecessary to carry any methylated spirits or
priming paste. However, some manufacturers recommend that
priming paste should be used for safety reasons, as liquid primers
can run down the side of the stove resulting in a danger of setting
alight the groundsheet if inclement conditions have forced you to
cook inside the tent.

Many models are self-pressurizing, the heat generated during

A selection of pressure stoves. From left to right: multi-fuel stove, petrol
stove, petrol burner on standard fuel bottle, compact stove with pan.

priming and subequent ignition keeping the fuel vaporized. Such self-pressurizing models can be slow to light in cold conditions and must be insulated from the ground if they are to work at all competently. This problem can be overcome by fitting special pumps which replace the filler cap, although these are not available for all models.

The fuel is readily available and, while these stoves work best with unleaded petrol or the more expensive special camp-stove fuel, they will operate fairly efficiently on low-octane fuel (i.e. two-star petrol), although there will inevitably be a slow build-up of lead which will eventually block the jet. Four-star petrol is not recommended as its use results in the jet becoming blocked with lead with monotonous regularity to the extent that the stove becomes very inefficient. Apart from the inconvenience, constant 'pricking' is not good for the jet which will soon become too large and need replacement.

A further disadvantage is that any fuel which is accidentally spilled will be highly flammable, even though it will evaporate fairly rapidly. For this reason refuelling should always be done well away from the tent, for if a stove is refuelled inside a tent, it is possible for any petroleum vapour resulting to explode when the stove is lit. Do not forget that the vast majority of camping injuries are burns and scalds.

*Multi-fuel pressure stoves*
Surprising as it may seem, there are pressure stoves available which purport to burn any liquid fuel, from methylated spirits to diesel! One or two of these are extremely efficient, but others are fairly complex and need 'setting up' in a different way for each type of fuel. All are expensive.

Multi-fuel stoves may be useful for extended trips to areas where you cannot guarantee to obtain any one fuel. However, their initial high cost means that most people will prefer to use some other type of stove which, although less expensive, will not necessarily be any less functional.

If you do buy a multi-fuel stove, make sure you read the manufacturer's instructions very carefully before using it for the first time.

Methylated spirits stove. This model comes complete with its own cookset.

*Methylated spirits stoves*

Gone are the days of the old-fashioned 'picnic stoves' which ran on meths. Although it is still possible to buy such models, there are far more efficient stoves available nowadays. Some of the best are compact units which come complete with their own set of nesting pans and this means you are buying not just a stove but also a complete set of pans and, with certain models, a small kettle as well. Such stoves can be an extremely attractive proposition for the first-time buyer.

One of the benefits of this type of stove is that they tend to thrive on draughts! Indeed, most of the flame control is done simply by turning the ventilation holes in the base towards or away from any draughts. They are simple to use, there are no jets which could become blocked and, because they require no priming, they are extremely convenient and give immediate maximum heat. Any fuel which is accidentally spilled will evaporate quickly. However, when compared to gas and liquid pressure stoves, the flame control is not that wonderful, they have a relatively low heat output and the fuel (which is heavy) burns very quickly. This means you have to carry a fair amount of fuel with you on the longer trips, and this in itself can pose problems as methylated spirits tend to 'creep' and therefore require a fuel container with a tight-fitting seal. Methylated spirits can also make the base of your pans sooty.

Refuelling, too, can cause problems. It has to be done on a regular basis and needs the utmost care. Methylated spirits burn with an almost invisible flame and accidents have occurred when people have mistakenly poured fresh fuel into a burner which was still alight.

GETTING TO KNOW YOUR STOVE

Even though gas and methylated spirits stoves are simple to use, it is important that you get to know your stove *before* you go camping in wild country. This is particularly important with pressure stoves as the lighting procedures will vary from model to model and it is all too easy to get a 'flare' if you are not used to it. Some of the more solidly built pressure stoves have a personality all of their own and different stoves of the same model can often seem to behave differently!

Use your stove to cook yourself a meal in the comfort of your kitchen. Particularly if it is a pressure stove, it might be advisable to light it a couple of times in the back garden first! Once you have cooked a meal inside with reasonable success, try doing the same thing outside on a windy night and see what a difference it makes. Do not forget that when you use your stove for real, not only might you be cold and tired but the weather could be so horrendous that you are forced to cook in the relatively cramped conditions of your tent. Yet it is in exactly these situations that you will need your stove to operate smoothly. During a stormy night in a tent, there is nothing quite so calming as the friendly purr of a pressure stove signalling an imminent brew.

FUEL CONTAINERS

If you are using a gas stove, you should not be faced with too many difficulties when it comes to transporting the fuel, apart from that of bulk. Empty containers take up just as much space as full containers, and empties should always be taken back to civilization. If you have enough space to take them into the wilderness, there is absolutely no reason at all why you should not take them back out again. With resealable cartridges it may be useful to mark the one being used, although half-used cartridges can be identified by weight.

If you have a stove which uses a liquid fuel you will obviously need a container in which to carry it. No matter what the type of liquid fuel, it is important that it is stored and carried in a container which will not puncture or leak. Plastic containers are generally unsuitable, no matter how well the lid fits, and it is far better (and safer) to buy an aluminium fuel bottle designed specifically for this purpose. Such bottles should have deeply-threaded necks into which a screw-cap can be firmly tightened. The better models have replaceable washers and optional safety pouring caps.

WINDSHIELDS

With the possible exception of those running on methylated spirits (in which the burner is usually totally enclosed), most stoves are highly susceptible to draughts. This applies most particularly to gas stoves where not only can the flame be easily blown out but the heat can be dissipated to such an extent that it takes hours to boil even a small amount of water. Although it is possible to buy windshields which fit around the burners of some models (indeed, some have a windshield as an integral part of the burner), these are not always as effective as they could be and you will often need to rig up some form of windshield yourself.

Draughtshields or windbreaks can be constructed from virtually any available material, the form they take being limited only by your imagination. In rocky terrain you can build low walls, any holes being plugged with earth; in other areas you can use a rucksack or construct something from sleepmats or survival bags. Some people carry fairly large pieces of kitchen foil which they use

A selection of cooking pans. From left to right: 5" billy can with lid, cookset, army-style mess tins.

in conjunction with long tent pegs. Making a windbreak from foil has the added advantage that it reflects heat but you must be careful not to enclose the stove completely. Particularly with gas or pressure stoves, this can lead to a build up of heat to such an extent that it can cause an explosion.

COOKING UTENSILS, ETC.
Unless you have bought a stove which comes complete with its own set of pans (such as certain models of gas stoves and most of the better spirit stoves), you will need something in which to cook your food. Aluminium is the best material as it is light and reasonably durable, and you will probably not do much better than to buy a standard cookset. These are available in a variety of sizes to suit different groups and there are also versions suitable for solo campers. You can even buy non-stick versions! The alternative is to buy a set of nesting 'dixies' (billycans), or – particularly useful for solo use – a set of army-type mess tins. The only other item of cooking paraphernalia which you might choose to buy is a small fish

Camping cutlery and crockery. Clockwise from back left: plastic mug, metal mug with plastic rim, deep plastic plate, deep plastic bowl, cutlery clip-set with pouch.

slice, although many people do without. It really all depends on what you intend to cook. Serving and cooking spoons are totally unnecessary unless you are cooking for a huge party; dessertspoons work just as well.

Unless you intend to eat straight from the pan or use spare lids and pans as plates and bowls (thus keeping the weight of your sack to a minimum), you are going to need some form of crockery. Perhaps the best idea is to use a large, deep plastic plate which can act as soup bowl, dinner plate and dessert dish. Many people take a large plastic mug (insulated versions are good even if slightly heavier), although this is really an unnecessary item if you also have a flask because you can simply use the mug which comes with the flask.

Bendy plastic crockery is fine but plastic cutlery tends to be too easily broken to be at all practical. Compact and fairly light metal cutlery sets (in which the knife, fork and spoon clip together) are available, the only additional 'eating tool' that might be found useful being a teaspoon.

Last but not least, you are going to need something with which to light your stove. Even if you have an ultra-modern stove with automatic ignition, it is unwise to rely solely on this. A good cigarette lighter (whether you smoke or not) is a useful thing to have, but don't forget that a lighter without any fuel is useless. This is not too much of a problem if you have a petrol lighter and a petrol pressure stove, but remember that lighter flints will not work if they are wet. Waiting for a flint to dry when you are dying for a brew is extremely frustrating, and many people prefer to take matches. These, too, can obviously be affected by damp, and although it is possible to buy waterproof matches (lifeboat matches) these are expensive. In any case, it is fairly easy to make your own. Simply get some non-safety matches and dip the heads deeply in either varnish or molten candlewax. When dry, store the matches head-down in a plastic film canister or a similar, waterproof container, and glue some sandpaper to the inside of the lid (Fig. 25). If you do this it is important that you store the matches head-down otherwise you run the risk that they could accidentally ignite on the sandpaper whilst in your rucksack or pocket!

Details of food containers, water carriers, etc. will be found in Section 1.5 and a discussion on cooking safety in Section 2.5.

## 1.5   Bits and pieces

The equipment described so far represents what can be considered as the bare essentials for camping in wild country. With a tent, a sleeping bag, a stove and a pan, together with your standard hill-walking kit, you could quite happily survive for a few days – always assuming, of course, that you have food and are in relatively close proximity to a water supply. In this section we are not so much concerned with mere survival as with comfort. With the possible exception of some form of water carrier, none of the items described below are essential, but many will help to make your life that much easier and the camping experience more pleasurable.

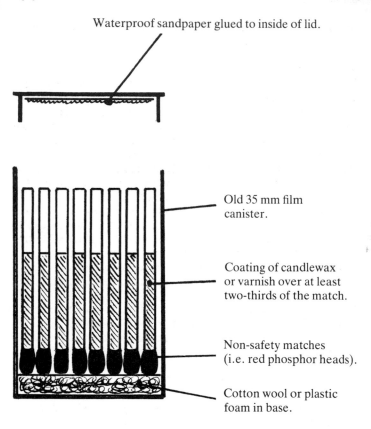

Waterproof sandpaper glued to inside of lid.

Old 35 mm film canister.

Coating of candlewax or varnish over at least two-thirds of the match.

Non-safety matches (i.e. red phosphor heads).

Cotton wool or plastic foam in base.

**Fig. 25. Home-made waterproof matches.**

A few experienced campers may be surprised at some of the items I have described, whilst others may feel I have neglected to mention a piece of equipment which they consider to be essential. I make no apology for this, for it is as it should be. Camping in wild country, like all other forms of mountain and wilderness activities, is very much what you make it. The things I find exhilarating, others may find mundane, and vice versa.

WATER CARRIERS

Unless you are travelling through an area where you are sure to get water at almost any time, you will find some form of water carrier almost essential. Even if you camp close to a stream or lake, trekking backwards and forwards with any spare mugs or pans is far less convenient than having a container of water close to hand, especially if you decide to make a brew in the middle of the night. That being said, water is heavy, and you should try to plan your camps so that they are sited within a reasonably short distance of some form of water supply (see also Section 2.4).

Water containers come in a wide variety of shapes and sizes. For use whilst on the move, those metal or plastic containers with capacities of up to 1 litre will be found most useful. The lighter they are, the better, for a litre of water weighs approximately 1 kilogram. Whether you choose one which can clip to your belt or one which fits inside a pocket of your rucksack is entirely up to you. Personally I prefer the latter as I find a container of slurping water swinging from my waist most off-putting. Either way, make sure that the container has an effective seal and a strong, well fitting cap which cannot loosen accidentally. The better aluminium bottles, for example, have deeply-threaded necks and replaceable sealing washers.

One further consideration is that the container must be designed to take drinking liquids. Certain plastic containers will make water taste foul, whilst some metal bottles are designed specifically for fuel. Although you can use an unlacquered aluminium bottle for pure water, you must not fill it with fruit juice or any other mixture. If you want to carry fruit juices with you, your best bet is to buy a lacquered metal container.

Fuel bottles and water bottles should be readily and easily distinguished; apart from the obvious dangers of having a swig of meths or filling your stove with water, drinks which are flavoured with petrol or paraffin will not do much for your taste-buds! Keep the containers separate and never use a water bottle for fuel or vice versa.

You will not want to cart around a large plastic jerrycan, so look for collapsible or roll-up water containers which are obtainable in varying capacities. These may be found useful in base camp situations, where your nearest water supply is some distance from your camp site, or if you are simply feeling lazy! Although the better models are fairly sturdy, it is best not to drop them when full, to keep them away from stony ground and, when collapsed and packed in your rucksack, well away from sharp objects such as tent pegs.

WATER PURIFICATION

Unless you are camped high on a mountain or by an unmistakable spring, in which case you can be reasonably sure that the water is OK to drink, it pays to treat all water supplies with a modicum of suspicion. Water purification tablets are very useful: they are light and simple to carry, and easily obtainable. However, some take a long time to work, most give the water an unpleasant taste, and none that I know of will get rid of any chemical impurities.

Boiling is another answer although, again, this may not get rid of any chemical impurities. Purifying your water by this method is also time-consuming and will burn up your fuel supplies, as to be effective you need to boil the water fairly vigorously for at least five minutes.

Finally, if you go camping in wild country on a regular basis, you might like to consider purchasing a water filter. These come in an increasing number of shapes and sizes: some are totally unsuitable for wild country use (being heavy, bulky and/or incredibly slow) and others are little more than straws (fine if you are alone and surrounded by muddy, contaminated puddles but of little use on a wilderness camping trip). In my opinion, few if any are worth the cost and effort involved.

FOOD CONTAINERS

If you are spending several days away from civilization, a fair proportion of the weight you carry will consist of food supplies. Bearing this in mind, a surprising amount of weight (and space) can be saved by taking the food out of its original packaging and

A selection of useful containers. From left to right: 35mm film canister, plastic screwtop jars, aluminium fuel and water bottles, plastic water bottles, and (in front) a roll-up water carrier.

repacking it. Whilst the food itself will be discussed in detail in Section 2.3, it will be useful to look at various containers and methods of packing.

First and foremost, it is both totally unnecessary and potentially dangerous to carry glass containers with you for they are both heavy and fragile. It is far better to use plastic containers and the very useful and ubiquitous polythene bag. The larger plastic containers are more reliable if fitted with screwtops rather than snap-on lids which have the unfortunate habit of coming off at the most inconvenient times. Plastic bags are better knotted or sealed with sticky tape than wire ties, the metal of which can puncture the bag allowing the contents to escape over everything. Most sticky tape is not resealable, so make sure that you only fill each bag with enough for one serving. Alternatively, you can make use of small resealable plastic bags.

The contents of heavy, bulky tins can often be transferred to more suitable containers with a little thought. However, if you do take tins, don't forget the tin-opener. This does not have to be a bulky device – you can buy small and very effective baby tin-openers from most good gear shops, and you may well have a suitable blade on your knife (see p. 89).

Also useful for a number of purposes are 35 mm film canisters, airtight snap-lid pill containers (available from your local friendly chemist – make sure you wash them out!), and refillable plastic tubes (available from camping and outdoor shops).

LIGHTING

The form of lighting you choose will depend not only upon your budget but also on such factors as length of stay, time of year and any additional activities in which you may be involved whilst camping.

Perhaps the most useful form of lighting is a head-torch. Particularly useful, if somewhat expensive, are those models in which the battery is carried at the back of the head, the beam adjusts from a spot to a wide angle, and spare bulbs – either long-life, halogen or standard – can be stored in the lamp housing. Head-torches are useful for a number of reasons, the two most obvious being that they leave your hands free and that the beam follows where you are looking. If you are visiting wild country in winter conditions, you would be well advised to take a head-torch with you as a standard piece of equipment.

If you decide you would prefer a hand-held torch, it is better to choose one which is waterproof and durable, with a good beam. Some of the mini-torches now available are virtually indestructible and come complete with xenon bulbs which give an amazing amount of light.

Whatever type of torch you buy, you will find it far better to use alkaline batteries. Although these are heavier than normal batteries, their extended life and reliability mean you will have to carry less weight in the long run. However, batteries are no good if

Lighting. From left to right: long-life candles, waterproof torch, zoom head-torch, sturdy pen-torch with xenon bulb.

they are flat, and you should make sure that the torch cannot become accidentally switched on whilst in your rucksack. Torches which you screw up to turn on are safer than those with buttons or switches but, in any case, you would be wise to store torch and batteries separately, or to load the batteries incorrectly. One word of caution – make sure you do not short-circuit the terminals on alkaline batteries (easier to do with flat-shaped batteries than with the more common cylindrical ones) as this could cause them to leak caustic material. Remember, also, that batteries do not like cold weather. Particularly in winter it may be advisable to keep the batteries (or even the complete torch) in your sleeping bag at night.

Candles are another good form of lighting. In addition to giving a surprising amount of light (especially when used in conjunction with a reflector made of silver foil), they also give off a certain amount of heat. However, naked flames and tents can be a dangerous combination, so make sure that lit candles are kept well away from

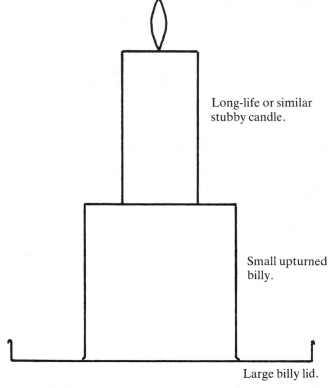

Long-life or similar
stubby candle.

Small upturned
billy.

Large billy lid.

**Fig. 26. Candle placed on billy can.**

the walls or roof. Although it is possible to buy very light and
compact candle-lanterns which reduce the risk of fire, these
represent extra weight which you have to justify. Far better,
perhaps, to use stubby, long-life candles which are less likely to fall
over, even though these are heavier than standard candles. If these
are placed on top of a small upturned billycan, any accidental knock

will probably result in them going out before they hit the groundsheet. Placing them or the upturned billy on a frying pan or large billy lid is even less hazardous (Fig. 26).

For general wild country camping, gas lanterns and pressure lanterns are generally too heavy and cumbersome to be of real benefit. However, during extended trips or in situations where there is a permanent base camp, these may be found suitable (see section 2.6).

WASHING AND CLEANING

Personal hygiene is no less important during camping trips in wild country than during normal life. Indeed, many people will tell you it is more important. What would be regarded as a minor stomach upset when in the comfort of your own home can become a serious problem if you are several strenuous miles from the nearest habitation.

Whilst you obviously need not go over the top with washing-bags full of anti-perspirants, deodorants and such like, a toothbrush, a hairbrush or comb, and some soap probably represent the minimum kit. Biodegradable soap is now widely available and is infinitely preferable to normal soap as it is 'ecology friendly'. This can also be used to wash socks or other items of clothing on the longer trips (see also Section 2.6). Nor need you carry a bulky towel which, in any case, will become heavy when wet. Light, compact and effective 'camping towels' (which work by capillary action) are now available from most outdoor shops. These take up very little space and dry extremely quickly.

Cleaning cooking pans (other than the non-stick varieties) is best done with a soap-filled wire-wool pad, the process being made that much easier if you soak the pans with water immediately you have finished cooking. There are few jobs more horrendous than arriving at a camp site late in the day only to find that you have to scrub the hardened and incredibly stubborn remains of breakfast from your pans before you can start the evening meal! Alternatively, you might like to use one of those small sponges which has one side covered with a scouring pad. Apart from cleaning non-stick cooking utensils and suchlike, the sponge is extremely useful for mopping up

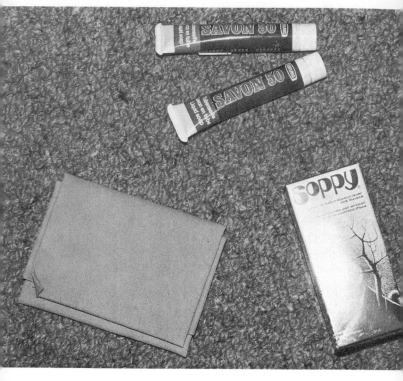

Washing and drying! Clockwise from top: tubes of biodegradable soap, special soap for down sleeping bags, compact camping towel.

accidental spillages, leaks and general dirt, particularly from the inside of the tent. If there are a lot of you, a tea-towel will also be useful.

Finally, don't forget the toilet paper. If you are only going for a short trip, there is no need to take a whole roll (even though soft toilet tissue, being absorbent, has a variety of uses). Whilst it is not strictly necessary to dig a latrine for single overnight stops, faeces should be buried and used toilet paper burnt, the resulting ash being buried with the faeces.

## FIRST AID
A small first aid kit is regarded as a standard piece of equipment for all mountain or moorland walking and it is advisable to take a slightly more comprehensive kit during camping trips in wild country. Foot care, in particular, becomes increasingly important the further you are from habitation or the longer you intend to stay in the wilds. In addition to the usual selection of plasters, bandages and general dressings, you should include some form of treatment for minor burns and scalds (the most common form of camping injury), and you might like to consider taking an insect repellent that contains a high percentage of diethyltoluamide. In certain areas at certain times of the year, biting insects can make camping feel like purgatory!

Certain acquaintances of mine would not contemplate camping in wild country without carrying both indigestion tablets and some form of relief from stomach upsets. Whilst, in these particular cases, the inclusion of such items doubtless has much to do with a lack of cooking prowess, you may like to consider them, especially if you are unfortunate enough to be prone to these complaints.

## ODDS AND ENDS
*Silver foil* has already been mentioned on a number of occasions and it has countless uses around the camp site. Apart from the fact that it reflects heat and light and can be used to form a windbreak, it is also useful as wrapping material.

If insect repellent is needed, *mosquito coils* will be appreciated. Whilst they tend to have a limited effect if left to smoulder in the open, they can be very effective if placed in the entrance of the tent, between the inner and the flysheet.

*Plastic bags* are extremely serviceable for a number of reasons. Apart from storing food and other items, they can also be used to keep dry items dry and wet items wet, as well as separating the two! Large plastic bags can be used as waterproof liners inside your rucksack; bin liners being the obvious choice. However, unless you are very careful these tend to puncture rather too frequently, and you may prefer to buy special heavy-duty plastic rucksack liners which will certainly last slightly longer.

You may also like to take a length of *paracord* or light nylon line. This makes very good emergency guy line or bootlace, can be used to form a washing-line, to construct a shelter on those nights when

Various odds and ends. Paracord, insect repellents, baby tin-opener, small pocket knife, mosquito coils.

you don't want to sleep in the tent, and for a hundred and one other purposes.

If you take paracord, you will also need something with which to cut it (although you can burn it apart). In any case, a small *penknife* can be a very useful object, especially if it contains such things as a tin-opener. If you do decide to buy such a tool, it is infinitely better to choose a good quality knife with a few blades than to go for a poorer quality, heavy monstrosity with countless, blunt blades which break on the first occasion you try to take a boy scout from a horse's hoof (or whatever it should be). Joking aside, a poor quality knife with blades which are difficult to sharpen is more of a liability than a help; you are far more likely to injure yourself on a blunt knife than one which is razor sharp, simply because of the force needed and the frustration caused.

A basic *tent repair kit* can be worth its weight in gold, enabling you to repair an accidentally punctured groundsheet or small tear on the spot, before it becomes a hazard. If your tent uses rubber rings as peg attachment points, it would be wise to include a couple of these as they can snap without warning.

Some people never go camping without taking a small, *inflatable pillow* with them. Most people will regard this as a luxury, being perfectly content to lay their heads on spare clothing or suchlike, but if the absence of such an item results in sleepless nights it is undoubtedly worth taking.

I never go camping without taking a *notepad* and *pencil*, and a *camera* with plenty of *spare films*. Whilst the former items in particular are merely a personal foible, there is no doubt that they have their uses, and if you possess a camera, I can almost guarantee you will wish you had it with you if you leave it behind!

Last but by no means least, if you are camping in winter conditions you will find a small *snow shovel* a great asset. In summer months, a small *trowel* will also be found useful for burying faeces or digging grease pits, etc.

Do not forget that I make the assumption that you are already a fairly experienced walker, reasonably well versed in mountaincraft. As such, you will obviously realize that the bits and pieces described in this section are in addition to your normal outdoor clothing and equipment. Everything you would normally take on a day's walk in rough terrain should be carried with you when you camp. If such items can fulfil a dual role, thus keeping down the amount of weight carried, so much the better.

## 1.6  Carrying it all

Two of the most important considerations in wild country camping are weight and bulk. Not only are you going to have to carry everything on your back but you also have a limited amount of space in which to pack it. On any expedition, but particularly those undertaken during winter conditions when you will need comparatively more gear, you will have to think very carefully about what you are taking and why. Your load should never exceed one-third of your body weight and, unless you are disappearing into the back of beyond for more than a few days, rarely need it be more than about 20 kilograms.

When it comes to carrying it all, there is really no alternative to a good quality, purpose-designed rucksack. As with everything else in this sphere of activity, you will find, certainly on first glance, that there appears to be a vast assortment of shapes, sizes and models from which to choose. Although much of the choice will be purely a matter of personal preference, it will be helpful to discuss some basic principles of rucksack design and to look at the pros and cons of various types.

TYPES OF RUCKSACK

First and foremost, beware of cheap models where quality has been sacrificed for the sake of economy. As you should, by now, be aware, good equipment is not cheap, and the quality of your rucksack is just as important as the quality of your tent. There is little point, for example, in buying a rucksack which has poorly finished seams which split as soon as you try to cram in your gear, or where the straps are so weakly attached to the main body that they come apart after a few hours of scrambling over rough terrain. Similarly, unless your rucksack is comfortable when fully loaded, it is not going to do much to help you enjoy your trip.

However, it is only fair to point out that there are a number of very competitively priced and eminently suitable rucksacks available. Whilst it would, perhaps, be invidious to single out any particular make or model, it is luckily fairly easy to tell the good from the bad and, in any case, your local, friendly gear retailer should be able both to advise you and show you a range of suitable models. Good indicators of quality are heavy zips to pockets, wide and well padded shoulder straps (although these may be narrower in rucksacks which have well designed, load-bearing hip belts (see page 94)) and, particularly important, well stitched seams, especially in areas of stress such as at strap and hip belt attachment points. Additionally, such rucksacks will be simple in design, reasonably easy to adjust (possibly whilst on your back) and will have a minimum of external straps and pockets.

When you boil it down to basics, there are really only two alternatives: framed high packs and anatomical rucksacks. Although the former have been replaced to a large extent by the latter, framed high packs still have their devotees and a brief description will not go amiss.

*Framed high packs*
Framed high packs consist essentially of two separate parts: an aluminium or light alloy frame and a totally independent sack. The frame can either be in the shape of an H or can be 'booted', i.e. have a further cross-member along the base. This cross-member is often extended to form a useful platform on which it may be possible to strap a stuff sack, sleepmat or some similar item. In some models, the platform is designed in such a way that the frame is free-standing. Obviously, the more metal there is, the heavier will be the frame.

Whatever its design, the frame should be shaped to fit the curve of your back, and the individual tubes should either be welded together or held in place by screwed plastic compression joints. The former method results in a rigid structure which requires no maintenance (but is difficult to repair), whereas the use of compression joints results in a cheaper frame in which the joints should be periodically checked for tightness.

The shoulder straps and padded hip belt are usually attached to the frame by means of metal rings or nylon straps, as is the sack itself. In its most basic form, this will simply be a large bag of either lightweight nylon proofed with polyurethane or heavier 'cordura' (a man-made canvas-like material), which usually tapers out from the base and has a large flap of material big enough to cover the top. In more expensive models, this bag may be divided into two compartments, one above the other. The baffle between each compartment is often removable, held in place either by a zip or by tapes, and the bottom compartment is accessible from the outside by means of a zipped opening. Additionally, there may be two, fairly large external pockets (removable in some models), and a pouch or boxed pocket in the top flap. Provision for equipment tapes and a haul loop, plus elasticated edging to the top flap completes the scene.

On some framed high packs it is possible to use the sack without the frame; this can be useful on longer expeditions where the sack itself can be used as a day sack or climbing sack. In yet other models there may be compression straps at either side, enabling you to alter the capacity of the sack. These straps can also be convenient for carrying such things as short ski-mountaineering skis.

*Anatomical rucksacks*

With the possible exception of those situations in which unusually heavy loads have to be carried, framed high packs have largely been replaced by anatomical rucksacks. These are basically the sack part of the framed high pack with an integral internal frame and a very substantial and well padded, built-in hip belt system. Models are available with either a variety of harness sizes (the harness being the complete shoulder strap/hip belt system), or will be fully adjustable to fit different people. Some models allow for 'on-the-back' adjustment, some come complete with lumbar pads, whilst others come in male and female versions to allow for anatomical differences.

The sack part of anatomical rucksacks is virtually identical to that of framed high packs except that it is generally narrower. In its most basic form it consists of a simple bag, but more often it comes complete with two side pockets (or has provision for these to be fitted) and a top pouch pocket. Models are available either with or without a bottom compartment, this usually being separated from the main body of the sack by a removable baffle. Haul loops tend to be fitted as standard, and usually there are equipment loops for carrying ice axes, etc. Some models have document pouches and small zipped pockets for valuables (useful for car keys, etc.), and many have compression straps.

When correctly fitted, such a rucksack tends to be very stable and extremely comfortable. However, many models hug the body so tightly that it is impossible for perspiration to evaporate, and this can lead to wet backs. Many such rucksacks are fitted, therefore, with a form of padded ribbing in an attempt allow some ventilation to take place. This tends to be more effective in some models than in others.

## CHOOSING A RUCKSACK

There are several factors which should be taken into consideration when choosing your rucksack, the most important being that it should fit correctly and be comfortable in use. A good rucksack will 'feel right'. With a framed high pack, the top of the frame should be level with your ears, the base comfortably against the small of the back, in line with the top of your hips. With an anatomical rucksack, the fit is even more important, and you should make sure that the shape of the internal frame mirrors that of your back. The easiest way to check this is to put on the sack and look in a mirror. Make sure, also, that the hip belt fits comfortably around the top of the hips (*not* around the waist). Generally speaking, hip belts on anatomical rucksacks are worn slightly higher than those on frame high packs, the latter fitting around the hip bones themselves.

Buying an anatomical rucksack is very similar to buying a pair of boots because the fit is of the utmost importance. Additionally, anatomical rucksacks will often need breaking in to allow the internal frame to bend slightly to your shape. On certain models this bending may need a little help but such adjustments should be minimal, most of the movement occurring naturally over the first

Friendly retailer posing in order to demonstrate the correct fit of an anatomical rucksack!

few trips. You may experience some initial tenderness around the hip bones and possibly, to a lesser extent, around the shoulders, but this should soon disappear.

Whatever the type of rucksack, it should fit on your back in such a way that the main loading bears directly on to the pelvic girdle through the hips. The shoulder straps, whilst sometimes taking up to about 40% of the weight (depending upon both the model and fit of the rucksack), are mainly there to stop the rucksack falling backwards and to keep the weight close to the body so it bears downwards on to the hips with a minimum of strain on the shoulders or spine. For this reason, you should do up the hip belt first, only then adjusting the shoulder straps.

One further factor which should be considered when choosing between framed high packs and anatomical rucksacks is any additional activity in which you intend to participate when away. Framed high packs, for example, are unsuitable for use when there is any rock-climbing, mountaineering or scrambling to be done, simply because the frame is too cumbersome and can easily become snagged on projecting rocks, etc. Anatomical rucksacks, on the other hand, tend to be very stable and compact, and apart from the fact that they are less likely to get in the way, they also tend not to alter the centre of balance to so great an extent. This being said, any rucksack which has a profusion of pockets and dangling straps is going to be a nuisance in such situations, so simplicity is often best.

The material from which your sack is made is largely a matter of personal choice, but the heavier canvas or cordura fabrics will obviously result in a heavier rucksack. For this reason, many people prefer lighter but less hardwearing nylon fabrics. Whatever the material, beware any claim that the rucksack is 100% waterproof. The material may be, but I doubt that the rucksack will be! Even if all the seams are taped and all the zips baffled, water *may* seep in through access flaps, especially in the wet and windy weather that can be experienced in the mountains, and in winter conditions spindrift can find its way into the most surprising of places. For this reason it is always advisable to use one or more waterproof rucksack liners of some description, and to pack such things as down sleeping bags and spare clothing in waterproof stuff sacks and/or plastic bags.

Finally, with regard to size, you should be looking for a rucksack with a capacity of between 60 and 75 litres. If you need a bigger sack you are either not very good at packing or you are carrying too much. The final choice is down to you and will probably be influenced by price, the size of your tent and sleeping bag, and the average length of time you intend to be away. Compression straps are useful here as they allow you to buy a larger sack and use it for both long and short expeditions. One word of warning: if you buy a sack that is too big, you will be faced with an almost irresistible temptation to fill it to capacity, with the inevitable result that you take along things which are totally unnecessary and are therefore useless weight. Far better, in this instance, to choose a rucksack that is slightly too small than one that is slightly too big.

## PACKING YOUR RUCKSACK

There is a certain art to packing a rucksack. Space is at a premium and you should think carefully about what is going to go where. Certain items, particularly such things as billycans and mugs, can be very wasteful of space, and you should try to fill these with smaller items rather than using up valuable space with a lot of voids.

While stuff sacks and plastic bags are useful for keeping several items together, compression sacks are even more useful when it comes to saving space. Compressible items such as sleeping bags and duvet jackets can be packed in compression sacks, often with a space saving of about 50%.

Packing should not be done in a haphazard way. Throwing in items as they come to hand is not going to result in a comfortable journey. You should plan your packing almost as carefully as you plan your trip. The main aim is to achieve a well balanced load with a good weight distribution, in which the heavier items are towards the top. In a well designed rucksack, this will help to ensure that the load bears directly on to the hips. You should also consider the order in which you are going to need the various items. Things that will be needed during the journey should be packed in an easily accessible position; on a day which promises rain, for example, you are not going to be very happy if you have to unpack your entire load simply to get at your waterproofs.

One of the standard ways to pack a rucksack is with the sleeping bag and spare clothing at the bottom (possibly in the bottom compartment, if your rucksack has one), and the tent and cooking equipment, together, perhaps, with some food, towards the top. Some compartmentalized rucksacks have baffles which are designed in such a way that you can put long tent poles down the inside of the sack, and with certain tents this can be a very useful feature. Remaining food, sundry items and possibly some drink can go in one of the side pockets, and stove fuel in the other.

Items needed during the day will usually go in a side pocket or the

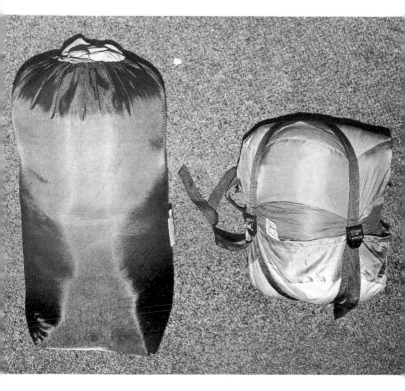

A compression sack can make a vast difference to the size of your sleeping bag.

top pouch, with waterproofs at the top of the main compartment. Your sleepmat can be strapped either to the top or bottom of your rucksack (many have facilities for straps at both ends), although some people unroll such sleepmats and use them as liners inside the rucksack. Emergency rations can go anywhere and your survival bag can be folded and used either as a waterproof base right at the bottom of the rucksack or as a liner along the back. Vacuum-packed

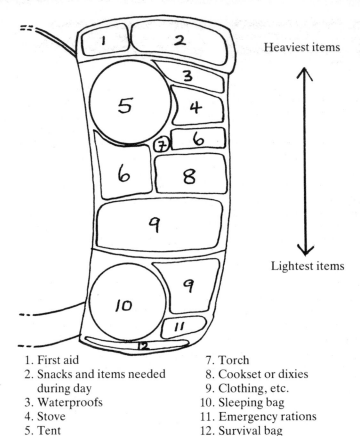

1. First aid
2. Snacks and items needed during day
3. Waterproofs
4. Stove
5. Tent
6. Food
7. Torch
8. Cookset or dixies
9. Clothing, etc.
10. Sleeping bag
11. Emergency rations
12. Survival bag

Other items, with the exception of your sleepmat which can either be strapped to the top or bottom of the rucksack or used as a liner, can be used to fill odd spaces or can go in the side pockets.

**Fig. 27. Example of a packed rucksack.**

survival bags are available, and although these are thinner than those normally bought, they take up very little space. Your first aid kit can go either in the main body of the rucksack or in the top pouch. An example of a typically packed rucksack is shown in Fig. 27.

Please note that the above description is only a suggestion and not a rigid rule. So long as you achieve a well balanced, comfortable load in which items which may be needed *en route* are relatively easily accessible, it does not really matter what goes where. There are, however, four points worth noting. Firstly, it is inadvisable (for reasons which become painfully obvious as you walk along) to pack items with hard or pointed edges towards the back of your rucksack. Secondly, you should ensure that your stove fuel is kept well away from foodstuffs. Thirdly, try to resist the temptation to strap numerous items to the outside of the rucksack as these will simply upset the balance and make the load unwieldy; and, finally, try to ensure that the heaviest items are packed towards the top.

POUCHES AND CAMERA BAGS

Many gear shops stock a wide selection of pouches, some of which can fit on the hip belt of your sack, whilst others hang round your neck or need a separate waistbelt. Some of these can be very useful for sundry items, especially those which would otherwise be easily lost or are needed at regular intervals. Such pouches come in various shapes and sizes, some being useful for guidebook, map and compass, others being more suited to day rations and occasional nibbles.

Particularly good for keen photographers are camera pouches designed to protect various items of photographic equipment from the elements (and from accidental bangs and scrapes), whilst leaving them readily accessible. While it is, of course, perfectly acceptable to pack a camera in the rucksack along witheverything else, I personally find it far more convenient to have it ready to hand at all times, and consider my camera pouch to be an almost essential item of equipment! As with rucksacks, however, such pouches should be comfortable, and if you dislike the idea of having such things strapped around your waist, it is pointless you buying them in the first place.

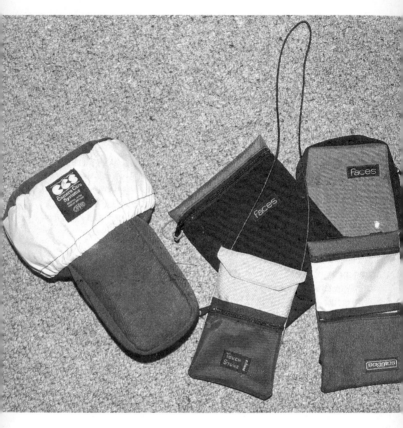

A selection of pouches.

**Part Two**

# The camping experience

## 2.1 Introduction

Spending two or more days in areas of wild country can be a totally different proposition to the odd day trip when you can return to the comfort and relative safety of a valley camp or other base each night. Particularly when the weather turns nasty, you will need a fair degree of mountaincraft in order to gain the maximum enjoyment from your trip. When carrying a heavy load, for example, such things as route finding and conservation of energy become even more important than during day trips. Likewise, a simple mistake in navigation which would not otherwise be too serious can, when camping, lead you to arrive late at your chosen site, perhaps even after dark, and this can make all the difference between a comfortable or uncomfortable night, no matter how good your equipment may be.

As with all other spheres of outdoor activities, the various skills which together make up campcraft cannot be taught in a book. The only way to learn is by gaining practical experience. If you have a few uncomfortable nights along the way, so be it; the pain will soon go but the experience will not be lessened.

In this part of the book we will be more concerned with the camping experience than with the use of the various items of equipment. The final choice of gear is entirely up to you and you will have to learn how to use it yourself. The camping experience, too, will mean different things to different people. Everyone will have their own approach, their own highlights, their own (perhaps peculiar) ways of solving little problems or making themselves more comfortable. Again, this is how it should be, for we are all individuals, and living in wild country with only the basics around us tends to bring out our individuality. A good example of this is the fact that you will very quickly find your choice of companion(s) can have a profound effect on the experience, especially if you are sharing a tent!

Wild country camping is essentially a personal affair so it is not an easy task to describe the camping experience with any great degree of objectivity. However, to my mind, there are several things which stand out as being important and in the following pages I have devoted a section to each of them. The first is planning and preparing for the trip, something which many people enjoy simply for the delightful sense of anticipation which it brings. Although it may not be strictly necessary to plan the trip in detail and many people prefer to shoulder their rucksack and set off into the wilds with little planning, some form of preparation is essential, certainly until you have gained a reasonable amount of experience.

Secondly comes eating and drinking, two activities which can become memorable experiences for both positive and negative reasons! Camp cooking, and particularly the evening meal, is an important part of wild country life and can make or break an otherwise mediocre trip. Apart from the fact that you are going to have to eat fairly well to supply the large amounts of energy you will often be using, you will probably have a voracious appetite and will look forward to your food. Luckily, you do not have to be a gourmet chef to produce good, tasty, basic camp food which supplies you with all the energy you will need in a very enjoyable way!

The third thing which stands out as being important is the siting of your camp. A good choice of site may well increase your enjoyment and an inappropriate choice may result in more than just discomfort. Particularly in bad weather conditions, choosing a suitable camp site can be of the utmost significance.

You may not like the idea to begin with but the need for some form of camp routine will become all too apparent during your early trips, particularly if the weather is poor. Although there are a few chores which have to be done and never get any more enjoyable, after only a few trips most of your routine will become so ingrained that you follow it automatically. It is, perhaps, at this stage that the skill of campcraft begins to evolve.

Wild country in the Brecon Beacons National Park. Choosing a well-sheltered site in such terrain requires careful thought.

To conclude this section I briefly discuss a number of very basic factors which should be borne in mind when contemplating longer expeditions, possibly taking place in more remote regions. However, by the time you feel ready to go off for days, perhaps even weeks at a time, you will most likely have had a reasonable amount of experience of camping in wild country, and will doubtless be able to think of many factors other than those discussed. I make no claim to total comprehensiveness – in this sphere of activity not only is that impossible, it is also undesirable.

## 2.2   Planning and preparation

One of the joys of wild country camping is the spontaneity of being able to stop and pitch your camp virtually anywhere you like. While some of the more experienced among you may simply drop a load of gear into a rucksack and head out into the wilds with only a rough idea of where you are heading, most people will want to do a certain amount of homework before setting out.

### BASIC RESEARCH

Although planning your trip down to the last detail is not strictly essential – indeed, some of the more experienced devotees of wild country camping may tell you that following a rigid itinerary detracts from the enjoyment of the trip – many of them would, I hope, agree that some form of planning or basic research is both necessary and desirable, particularly when visiting a new area. In any case, and certainly until you have had a reasonable amount of experience, you will find that a little planning goes a long way towards making your trip that much more enjoyable.

First and foremost, you have to decide where you are going to go. I have suggested a few areas which you might like to visit in Appendix I but it may be prudent to plan your first trip to an area which you already know from day walks. In any event, once you have made your choice (or at least narrowed it down to one or two areas), it will be helpful to find out as much as you can about the place. If you are a member of a walking or climbing club, there will probably be other members who will be able to help; your local

library, too, can be a useful source of information. If your chosen
area lies within a National Park, try writing to the Information
Officer who will doubtless be able to advise you and will probably
send you details of local guidebooks, National Park leaflets, etc.
(see Appendix V).

Some people go camping simply for the pleasure that it brings.
Others use camping as a means to an end, enabling them to visit a
particularly remote crag or cave, or to have a leisurely exploration
of an isolated peak without the constraint of having to rush there
and back in a day. Either way, reading about the area in question
will be very helpful, for it may give you an indication of potential
problems and will undoubtedly give you a certain amount of
background knowledge which should help you make the most of
your stay.

Once you have decided on an area, buy yourself a map,
preferably at a scale of 1:25,000, and try to get the feel of the place.
If you have a particular objective in mind, use your map to work out
what is the best route to follow in order to get there and try to
picture the place so that you can choose a likely spot to camp. If, on
the other hand, you are simply going off for a few days peace and
quiet, poring over the map in this way may well lead you to see
features of interest which you might otherwise have missed and you
may be able to work out a rough itinerary between them.
Alternatively, you might simply like to walk into the area and pitch
camp, using this as a base from which to explore. In this case, try to
select a fairly central spot where you think there may be a suitable
site for your camp. Further information on camp sites will be found
in Section 2.4.

Try not to be too ambitious, particularly on your first few trips.
You will be carrying a fair amount of weight and this could slow you
down more than you expected. Once you have decided upon a
rough programme, ask yourself whether you are fit enough,
whether your equipment is suitable, and whether you have
sufficient experience and expertise to complete and enjoy what you
have planned. Be honest with yourself! There is very little point in
going on an expedition unless you enjoy yourself, and if you are
permanently shattered not only will this detract from the

enjoyment, but it could also lead to some potentially hazardous situations.

ROUTE PLANNING AND SELECTION

You should plan and select your route in exactly the same way as you would when out for a day walk. However, it is important that you take into consideration the fact that you will be carrying more weight than usual and will therefore be moving more slowly. Conservation of energy, always a major consideration when visiting wild country, takes on a particular and important significance when you are camping. If you are unsure about how to plan or select a route, can I draw your attention to my previous book, *Mountain Navigation Techniques*, in which such things are discussed in more detail.

You should plan your route so that you arrive in the area of your chosen camp site in good time. This is particularly important in winter when darkness falls early. Aim to reach the site no less than an hour before dusk, preferably earlier, and take such timing into consideration when planning any subsequent walks between camps. Try to leave yourself plenty of daylight in which to choose the exact site, pitch your tent and sort out your gear in a leisurely fashion without having to rush. Pitching camp hurriedly in darkness, especially in deteriorating weather conditions, is a recipe for disaster. If it looks as if you are not going to reach your objective until after dark or if the weather takes a turn for the worse, do not be afraid to modify your plans accordingly. It is better to pitch camp too early than too late.

After you have been on a few trips, you will have a better idea of how long it takes you to pitch camp and, in any case, you will almost certainly have worked out some form of routine (see Section 2.5). This will undoubtedly save you a considerable amount of time and effort, and will be of great help on those occasions when you get the timing wrong.

PREPARATION

Whilst planning may not be essential, some form of preparation most certainly is. In extreme situations this may involve such things as training to get fit for a particular objective, obtaining permission to camp at a special site, and so on, but more usually it is simply a matter of checking gear and getting suitable supplies.

It is of little use arriving at a camp site in the middle of nowhere, only to find that you have left some essential item of equipment at home. Although I am not a great fan of lists, there is little doubt that a gear list of some description can be very useful (a fairly typical example is shown in Fig. 28). If you are camping with other people, not only can you share out the food, but you may be able to share certain items of equipment. There is, for example, little point in everyone taking a stove and dixies, and if you are sharing a tent, one person can take the inner tent, whilst another takes the flysheet, the poles and the pegs. The various combinations are infinite.

**Fig. 28. Example of a gear list.** The following is an example of a gear list for a high-level camp in winter conditions. Please note that the items listed are those which you should consider taking in addition to your normal mountain-walking gear (i.e. map and compass, whistle, waterproofs, survival bag, emergency food, ice axe and crampons, goggles, gaiters, boots, watch, mittens, spare clothing. etc.).

Four-season mountain tent
Four/five-season sleeping bag
Sleepmat
Stove & fuel
Waterproof matches/lighter
Cookset or billies
Plate, knife, fork, spoon, mug
Water-bottle
Rations
Tin-opener
Scouring pad

Small sponge
Head-torch/candles
Toilet requisites & towel
Toilet paper
Snow shovel
Extra clothing
Silver foil
First aid kit
Personal items (i.e. camera, etc.)
Odds & ends

SHARING EQUIPMENT

Up to a point, the larger the group, the more gear you will be able
to share. However, there comes a time when discarding gear
becomes counter-productive: a group of six people with one stove
and a solo canteen between them is not going to lead to sumptuous
eating! With larger groups it may be better to divide equipment into
'tent packs', in which each tent is equipped as a totally self-sufficient
unit. In such situations it is dangerous to make assumptions: make
sure that everyone has got what you think they have got. After an
arduous walk-in, I once arrived at a very remote site in Scotland
looking forward to my evening meal only to find that we had left the
fuel-bottle behind! My partner had taken the stove and had
assumed that I would take the fuel; I had taken the pans and had
assumed that he had taken the fuel. We both felt as guilty as each
other. Luckily there was a little fuel left in the stove and we had
brought a small, solid-fuel burner for emergencies, but we had to
walk out sooner than we had planned.

CHECKING EQUIPMENT

Preparation extends from making sure you have packed all the gear
you intend to take, to ensuring that it is all serviceable. It was
simply a lack of preparation that caused us to have such an
uncomfortable night in the incident I related in the Foreword. Had
we checked the tent beforehand, we would have discovered the
ill-fitting poles and shortage of pegs and could have done something
about it. In addition to checking tents, it is advisable to check that
your stove is working and that all your other gear is in a usable
condition. I once arrived at camp and opened my cookset to
discover the remains of the breakfast I had hurriedly cooked on the
last morning of a previous trip! It was not a pretty sight and, despite
the close and vigorous attention I gave it with a scouring pad, I
could still taste the mould in my brew.

When checking through your gear in this way, especially after you
have been camping a few times, see if there are any items which you
have never used. Unless these are emergency items or items for
which you have a specific use, you might as well discard them as
they simply represent useless weight. Consider, also, whether there

might not be any lighter or less bulky alternatives to gear which you consider to be essential, or whether one alternative item can be substituted in the place of two. A good example of this is that there is little point in taking a tin-opener and a clasp knife when a small pocket knife with an integral tin-opener would do in their place.

FIRST TRIPS

If you have never been camping in remote areas before, prepare yourself for the experience by making sure you get to know your tent and all the other equipment before you go. This does not necessarily mean that you have to camp in an official site or (with permission) in a farmer's field, but it would be wise to find out what you are letting yourself in for before striking out with a vengeance! Perhaps the best way to do this is by camping on the edge of a wild area, where the terrain is similar to that which you will meet on more ambitious trips but where help or shelter is closer to hand in the unlikely event of anything going seriously wrong. If, on the other hand, you have had some previous lowland camping experience and you want head into the wilderness straight away, try to persuade a more experienced friend to come with you. If they are already converted, they will probably jump at the chance!

## 2.3 Eating and drinking

Camp food can be all things to all men. At its most spartan it will consist of such things as nuts, dried fruits, cheeses, cold meats, etc., and although this can be tasty, enjoyable and nutritious, most people will want to get something hot into them in all but the most balmy of summer conditions.

Hot food can range from the sublime to the ridiculous. At its most horrendous it will consist of any number of ingredients sloshed into a pan, heated up and gobbled down, no matter what the taste. At the opposite end of the spectrum there is nothing to stop you enjoying a four-course meal starting with soup, followed by peppered-steak, new potatoes and french beans, then fresh fruit salad and cream followed by cheese and biscuits.

Cooking tends to be one of the central activities of camp life.

Apart from its importance from a nutritional viewpoint (more of which anon), most people will have ravenous appetites, and mealtimes tend to be very social occasions. Despite what you may have thought, read or experienced, camp food does not have to be a random conglomeration of tasteless ingredients, nor does it have to taste foul! So long as you bear in mind the constraints put upon you in terms of the facilities available (i.e. few pans, limited fuel, generally only one stove, etc.), it should be possible to produce meals which are as good as those eaten at home, especially once you have had some experience and have worked out some form of routine (see Section 2.5).

BASIC REQUIREMENTS

Whether you are using your camp as a base for some other activity or moving from site to site on a daily basis, you will undoubtedly be using up a fair amount of energy, all of which needs to be supplied and replaced. Additionally, you are going to have to carry your supplies with you, and if carrying all this weight uses up more energy than can be replaced, you are going to run into several problems, not least exhaustion. Taking the correct food is therefore vitally important, especially on extended trips (see also Section 2.6).

The ideal food will be light in weight, reasonably compact and quick and easy to prepare and cook. It will also help if it is appetizing! These foodstuffs should be of a type or in a form which can supply a large amount of energy for their weight, such energy being made available to the body not only easily, but also quickly and effectively. Despite their often evil reputation, some of the modern dehydrated foods are exceptionally good, and this is particularly true of those in which the ingredients have been prepared by freeze-drying. Unfortunately, freeze-dried foods also tend to be on the expensive side, and the ready-prepared, freeze-dried meals which are available from both specialist shops and supermarkets tend to vary in quality quite considerably. Such variations are usually in terms of the amount of energy available (i.e. the number of calories), size of portion, preparation times and general taste.

Whilst many pre-packed meals are very good, there can be little doubt that there are some diabolical concoctions available in which there is more goodness in the packaging than in the meal itself! That being said, many people will find that dehydrated foods in one form or another are so convenient that they will make up the bulk of their supplies. There is nothing wrong with this so long as you note the calorific values and make up any deficiencies by adding other ingredients.

NUTRITIONAL INFORMATION
Particularly when we are working heavily or under stress, our food needs to contain a number of essential ingredients if the body is to function at all efficiently. Not only must all these ingredients be present, but they should also be available in a balanced combination. Although in the context of wild country camping we need not concern ourselves with chronic malnutrition (unless you are going away for months at a time), you will find it useful to have a very basic background knowledge of the nutritional requirements of the human body. Any imbalance or lack of any essential nutrient will affect the functioning of the body, and this will almost certainly have some effect upon your performance or enjoyment during the trip.

*Fats*
Fats are important for a number of reasons. They are an extremely rich source of energy (far better, weight-for-weight, than carbohydrates) and they contain essential fat-soluble vitamins. They also make us feel full! Although experts appear to disagree as to whether there is a minimum daily requirement, it is recommended that at least 25% of your total calorie intake should be supplied by fats.

Fats take a long time to digest so their energy will not be made available immediately. Additionally, if you eat more fat than the body requires, the excess will be stored for possible use at a later date. Although this stored fat can be converted to energy, the process requires not only a fair amount of oxygen but also the presence of sufficient carbohydrate. This is one example of the importance of a balanced diet.

Major sources of fat include butter and margarine (80%) and cheese (33%). Other useful sources are meat fats, egg yolks and nuts.

*Carbohydrates*

Carbohydrates, which consist of sugars, starches and celluloses, can be regarded as the real energy-givers. In fact, they supply very little else. Although, weight for weight, they contain less energy than the fats, this energy is available almost immediately, and the conversion requires no oxygen. Whilst there is no recommended minimum daily intake, you would be wise to supply about half your energy needs through sugars and starches. Any excess will be converted to fat and then stored. Cellulose cannot be digested by the human body and passes through the digestive system chemically unchanged (see also under Fibre).

Although many people will nibble glucose sweets and other forms of sugars throughout the day, too large an intake of carbohydrates can be counter-productive. In very basic terms, any over-indulgence in glucose will upset the body's sugar balance leading to all sorts of problems. The advice, then, is not to go on a glucose binge! It is far better to have an adequate intake of all the carbohydrates from the outset rather than sudden large intakes of one particular type. The golden rule is 'little and often'.

Major sources of carbohydrates include cereals, fruits and most types of vegetables, plus milk, chocolate and sweets, cakes and biscuits, etc.

*Proteins*

Proteins are needed for growth and for the building and repair of muscle tissue. In the digestive process they are broken down into various amino-acids which are then used by the body to form muscle and other types of tissue. Proteins from animal sources are known as 'complete proteins' because they supply exactly the right proportion of amino-acids, and those from vegetable sources are known as 'incomplete proteins' because they usually have some degree of imbalance. Whilst the average adult needs about 75 grams of proteins each day, at least half of which should be complete, children and adolescents need far more. Vegetarians may need a higher intake in order to get a sufficient quantity of each amino-acid. Those amino-acids which cannot immediately be used are not stored as protein but are either converted to energy or stored as fat.

The major sources of complete proteins are dairy produce, eggs, meat and fish. One of the richest sources is cheese (up to 33%). Lean meats, particularly bacon and beef, contain up to 25%. Sources of incomplete proteins include pulses such as broad beans and dried peas (up to 20%). Other useful sources are eggs (12% complete), wholemeal bread (6% incomplete), milk (3% complete) and potatoes (2% incomplete).

*Vitamins*
Despite what some modern advertising can lead you to believe, a normal balanced diet will provide you with plenty of vitamins. In general terms, vitamins are needed in the various chemical reactions which take place within the body and are classified according to whether they are soluble in fat or water. Vitamins A, D, E, and K are fat soluble, whereas vitamin C and the vitamin B complex are water soluble. Water soluble vitamins are not stored by the body to any significant extent and, whilst deficiencies of these are unlikely to be so severe as to affect you markedly, long trips with an unbalanced diet may result in early symptoms of deficiency diseases, mainly displaying themselves in the form of mental depression and short temper.

The amount and combination of vitamins needed will depend upon the level of activity and during particularly arduous expeditions it may be prudent to take extra amounts of the vitamin B complex. These vitamins are essential in the conversion of carbohydrates into expendable energy, and they can also help stamina, as can vitamin E. Unless you have access to fresh fruit and vegetables, extra vitamin C may also be needed during extended trips as the body cannot store any reserves.

That being said, even the early stages of vitamin deficiency are very rare except on the most arduous and spartan of extended trips.

Although some people take multivitamins or increase their intake of both vitamin C and the B complex via pills, this is not usually necessary. Indeed, certain vitamins, particularly A and D, can be toxic in high concentrations!

Finally, many people have independently commented to me that a course of multivitamins started about a month before a proposed trip will act as a good insect repellent! Although I can find no scientific evidence to support this claim, it is possible that in such circumstances something in the perspiration is distasteful to midges. I mention this purely for interest!

*Minerals*
In addition to vitamins, the body requires a certain number of basic minerals in order to function efficiently. The quantities required are extremely small and adequate intake will almost certainly be supplied through your diet.

Of special interest in our context is one particular group of essential minerals known as the electrolytes. These can be lost through sweating, and on particularly arduous expeditions or in extremely hot weather it is essential that they be replaced. Any deficiency will manifest itself first as cramp and then – if not corrected – in severe muscle contractions. Although the best way to maintain an adequate level of the electrolytes is through a balanced diet, it is possible to buy special electrolyte replacement drinks which contain all the necessary minerals, often in combination with some glucose.

*Fibre*
Fibre has become an 'in' word over recent years, the basic lack of fibre in most western diets being blamed for numerous ailments. Apart from making us feel full, fibre is also important in the digestive process and helps us get rid of waste material.

Processed and refined foods often contain very little fibre. One of the immediate effects of a lack of fibre will be constipation and general discomfort, especially if you are unfortunate enough to suffer from haemorrhoids, a far more common complaint in devotees of outdoor activities that is generally realized.

Unprocessed cereal products such as bran and wholemeal bread can be useful if you suffer in this respect, as can raw vegetables.

FOOD REQUIREMENTS

Apart from the obvious necessity of following a balanced diet, you will be using a fair amount of energy when you are camping in wild country and all of this will have to be supplied by your food. Although different people have varying levels of metabolism, these variations are generally so small as to be negligible for our purposes. You should also be aware that training and fitness will make both your body and (in basic terms) your metabolism more efficient.

Living and working in wild country, you should aim at a balanced diet which supplies you with something in the region of 4,500 kilocalories of energy per day. More calories will be needed in extreme conditions of cold or when the tasks you perform are exceptionally strenuous.

As mentioned above, about 50% of this energy should be supplied in the form of carbohydrate and at least 25% in the form of fat. By consulting the table shown in Fig. 29 you should begin to get some idea of what these figures represent in terms of food.

DRINK REQUIREMENTS

No less important than food is drink. Indeed, some authorities will tell you that it is more important, for the body can survive unimpaired without food for far longer than it can survive unimpaired without drink.

An average person will consume in the region of 2.5 litres of liquid each day, some of this amount being made up of moisture contained in food. This figure represents the norm in ordinary life. When camping in wild country, undertaking strenuous physical exercise, far more liquid will be needed. As a general guide you will need to consume about 1 litre of water for every 1000 kilocalories of energy you use. Thus an average intake of about 4.5 litres should be regarded as essential and considerably more than this may be needed in extremely hot or dry–cold conditions. Dehydration is a far more common complaint than most people realize.

**Fig. 29. Nutrition table.** (All quantities are approximate.)

| FOOD | CALORIES/GRAMME | % PROTEIN | % CARBOHYDRATE | % FAT |
|---|---|---|---|---|
| Minced beef (cooked) | 3 | 24 | 0 | 21 |
| Corned beef | 3 | 24 | 0 | 18 |
| Dehydrated beef | 2 | 34 | 0 | 6 |
| Pork luncheon meat | 3 | 15 | 1 | 25 |
| Bacon (cooked) | 6 | 30 | 3 | 52 |
| Ham | 3 | 23 | 0 | 31 |
| Tinned sardines (drained) | 2 | 24 | 0 | 11 |
| Tinned tuna (drained) | 2 | 29 | 0 | 8 |
| Fresh egg | 1 | 13 | 1 | 12 |
| Dried egg | 6 | 47 | 4 | 41 |
| Cheddar cheese | 4 | 25 | 2 | 32 |
| Processed cheese | 4 | 23 | 2 | 30 |
| Potato powder | 4 | 8 | 80 | 0 |
| Carrot (dehydrated) | 3 | 7 | 81 | 0 |
| Baked beans | 1 | 6 | 19 | 3 |
| Pasta | 4 | 13 | 75 | 0 |
| Rice | 4 | 8 | 83 | 0 |
| Porridge oats | 4 | 15 | 79 | 0 |
| White bread | 3 | 9 | 51 | 0 |
| Wholemeal bread | 2 | 11 | 48 | 0 |
| Butter & margarine | 7 | 1 | 0.5 | 81 |
| Beef stock cube | 1 | 20 | 5 | 3 |

| FOOD | CALORIES/GRAMME | % PROTEIN | % CARBOHYDRATE | % FAT |
|---|---|---|---|---|
| Orange | 0.5 | 1 | 12 | 0 |
| Apple | 0.5 | 0 | 12 | 0 |
| Apple flakes | 4 | 1 | 92 | 0 |
| Tinned fruit cocktail | 1 | 0.5 | 20 | 0 |
| Whole milk | 1 | 4 | 5 | 4 |
| Dried skimmed milk | 4 | 36 | 52 | 1 |
| Evaporated milk | 1 | 7 | 10 | 8 |
| Condensed milk | 3 | 8 | 54 | 9 |
| Dried apricot | 3 | 5 | 67 | 0 |
| Dried date | 3 | 2 | 73 | 0 |
| Raisins | 3 | 3 | 77 | 0 |
| Dried coconut | 5 | 4 | 53 | 39 |
| Peanut butter | 6 | 28 | 17 | 49 |
| Milk chocolate | 5 | 8 | 57 | 32 |
| Honey | 3 | 0 | 82 | 0 |
| Jam | 3 | 1 | 70 | 0 |
| Brown sugar | 4 | 0 | 96 | 0 |
| White sugar | 4 | 0 | 99 | 0 |

Hot drinks are very important in cold weather as they can help to maintain the body's core temperature with very little expenditure of energy. They are also superb morale boosters.

BASIC MEALS

You will find it helpful to plan out your basic meals in advance. As well as breakfast you will want snacks to eat while on the move, plus a substantial evening meal. If you can stretch to a late night snack, so much the better.

Many people plan their trips in such detail that they pack each meal separately. If this is done it is an easy task to find, for example, the bag or container marked 'Saturday breakfast' and simply cook it. Although this method is very effective and useful if you intend to be away for more than a couple of nights, you need not go to such extremes on simple overnight camps. However, it is undoubtedly beneficial to do some form of planning.

*Breakfast*

Bearing in mind all that has been said in this section so far, you should realize that breakfast is a very important meal. Apart from anything else, it should refuel your body ready for what could be a long day of strenuous activity. Breakfasts with a high fat content are to be preferred, but remember that fatty foods take a long time to digest. Your first meal of the day should therefore be a reasonably leisurely affair and you should try to avoid any strenuous activity immediately afterwards.

Many people start with a bowl of cereal, muesli or porridge oats over which they pour boiling water, perhaps with the addition of a little condensed or dried milk and some sugar (brown sugar tastes infinitely better than white). They follow this with cheese and biscuits or perhaps some oatcakes. Personally, I find that there is little to beat the good old-fashioned British Breakfast; it is high in fat content and sets me up for the day. If you can get a friendly local butcher to cut your bacon for you, so much the better: get him to cut it thick. Sausages, too, are good (so long as they are eaten fairly soon), as are real eggs (which can be transported in rigid plastic egg containers), although many people take powdered egg. Fried bread will usually mop up any remaining fat, the whole meal being washed down with lashings of hot tea or coffee. There is no need to take cooking oil with you: butter or margarine (in refillable tubes) can be used for cooking as well as for buttering bread, adding to instant potato, etc.

*Day snacks*
As I have said before, the golden rule for day snacks is 'little and often'. It is far better (and more efficient) to nibble constantly than to stop at around midday and fill your stomach. However, depending upon your programme, it may well be beneficial to stop for twenty minutes or so for a brew. If you have a flask with you, this could be filled at breakfast time although purists may well prefer to use their stove.

The best day snacks consist of such things as 'trail mixes' and similar concoctions. You can buy these ready-mixed from an increasing number of sources but you may find it cheaper and more convenient to make your own. Ingredients such as nuts and raisins, flaked coconut, dried fruit, brown sugar, rolled oats, chocolate chips, candied peel, etc. are all readily available and can be mixed in varying proportions to give a tasty, nutritious and energizing snack.

Here again, your day snacks are largely a matter of personal taste, some people preferring to carry sandwiches or filled rolls, others feeling that their day is not complete without a tin of sardines and some fruit. As long as you remember that your day snacks should give your energy levels a boost, it does not really matter what you eat. However, it is worth noting that a long stop and a large meal will often break your rhythm and make you feel lethargic. This is simply because your metabolism will not be able to serve your digestive system and your muscles at the same time.

*Dinner*
Your evening meal represents the most important meal of the day and, except in unusually balmy conditions, should have at least one hot course. A fairly standard evening meal consists of a starter, followed by the main course (usually some form of stew based

around a dehydrated or freeze-dried package), followed by a hot or cold dessert, all washed down by plenty of hot drinks.

Soup makes an ideal first course. The number of dried soup mixes available is quite incredible and you can always increase the goodness and flavour by adding a stock cube or some gravy granules. Many people also add some butter or margarine and perhaps even some herbs. While you are eating this, your main course can be cooking.

The main course is usually based around dehydrated or freeze-dried ingredients, although some people will take small tins of mince or stew. It is fairly important that you appreciate the differences in preparation between dehydrated and freeze-dried foodstuffs: dehydrated foods need to be simmered for some time and freeze-dried foods are ready to eat within a few minutes of adding boiling water with little (if any) further cooking. They therefore represent a considerable saving in terms of both fuel and time, and are also far more convenient.

It is possible to buy ready-packed, eat-from-the-bag camping meals which are very useful when away for the odd night. However, most people will wish to prepare something a little more substantial and, looking at the ingredients of some of the 'instant meals', a little less artificial. This will be the case particularly during extended trips when stews will probably tend to predominate. In this case, your basic stew mix can be enhanced by the addition of herbs and spices, curry powder, dried vegetables, baked beans and so on. Many people use potato powder as a thickener, whereas others make mashed potato and add some butter or margarine or even some grated cheese. Cheese is recommended since it is both nutritious and adaptable. Quick-cook pasta and quick-cook rice are also very useful, weighing next to nothing and taking up relatively little space.

In addition to the above, it is a good idea to have some form of dessert dish. At its most basic this will consist of fresh fruit, although hot desserts are excellent, especially during cold weather. The most common forms of hot dessert are based around rice pudding or custard, usually with the addition of further ingredients such as apple flakes, honey or jam, brown sugar, condensed milk, tinned or fresh fruit, etc. Spices such as cinnamon and nutmeg also make the dish tastier.

Dinner is usually finished off with another brew, possibly with nibbles in the form of cheese and biscuits, sweet biscuits or chocolate. Some people take a hip flask so that they can have a nip of alcohol. There is nothing wrong with this (indeed, it can add a touch of luxury to the proceedings) but make sure that it is only a nip. In cold and inclement conditions, alcohol can increase the chances of hypothermia as it dilates the capillaries leading to increased heat loss.

*Late night snack*
You will undoubtedly find it pleasant to have some form of snack shortly before retiring. At its most simple this will consist of a hot drink – hot chocolate or a soup made from a stock cube are popular. Many people like to have a bar of chocolate or, perhaps, biscuits and cheese or some other light snack.

By now you will no doubt realize that it is the little things which make camp cooking more enjoyable and appetizing. Things like curry powder, stock cubes, herbs and spices, salt and pepper, honey, jam, condensed milk, apple flakes and brown sugar can be worth their weight in gold. Their weight is negligible, they take up very little space and can be easily carried in small pill boxes or film canisters.

That being said, what you eat is very much a matter of personal taste and preference, and as long as your food is nutritious and convenient to carry and prepare, it does not really matter what you take.

## 2.4   Camp sites
Choosing a good camp site is more of an art than a science. Many experienced campers will tell you that it includes such things as having a good view from the tent door! However, a good view is not of much use if your nearest water supply is 5 kilometres away, the ground beneath the tent is sloping and composed of sharp stones,

and the position is such that you are likely to be blown away if the wind increases.

Many authorities on camping and mountaineering will tell you that you must choose your site with safety in mind. While I would be the last person to disagree with this, safety should not be the be all and end all of the choice.

There can be little doubt that selecting a suitable camp site is one of the most important parts of campcraft. When visiting a new area, it is wise to start looking for a site fairly early in the day. If you happen upon a spot which looks ideal, it is probably better to stop early rather than push on in the hope of finding something better; good sites which fulfil all the criteria tend to be few and far between.

BASIC CRITERIA

A good camp site will be reasonably flat and level, with no bumps, tussocks or rocks to make sleeping uncomfortable. It should be within easy walking distance of a water supply at the same time as being well drained, and should provide a high degree of shelter from the prevailing wind. If you can find such a site which is well away from any path or offers good views then so much the better.

It is worth bearing in mind that the weather can change with frightening speed, particularly in wild and mountainous areas. You should therefore choose your site and pitch your tent with the worst in mind, preferably with the back facing the direction of the prevailing (or expected) wind. It is far easier to do this from the outset than to be forced to adjust the tent in the teeth of a storm which has blown up from an unexpected quarter.

MOORLAND SITES

On flat moorlands or high plateau areas it can often be difficult to find a site which offers a reasonable amount of shelter from the wind. If you intend to camp in this type of area, the only advice I can give is to make sure that you have suitable equipment (i.e. a tent which is designed to be stable in high winds) and to be observant. A low hummock, flattened ridge or spur can give a surprising amount of shelter; so, too, can boulders.

The ground on moorlands can often be peaty; you should try to avoid such areas whenever possible as peat tends to hold water and can therefore become very muddy in wet weather. This is particularly true of shallow basins. You may find that skewer pegs have little holding power, and it may be advisable to use angle pegs in their place or to make skewers more secure by placing rocks on top of them. If this is done, make sure the rocks are placed in such a way that they cannot chafe the guy line or material.

ROCKY SITES

If the ground is at all rocky, you will probably want to clear an area so that you can pitch your tent without being forced to lie on uncomfortable rocks all night. On high moorland sites where there may be little shelter from the wind, it may be worth your while to use the cleared stones (and others from the immediate areas) to build a low windbreak of some description. This is recommended when the weather is threatening or if you intend to stay at the same site for more than one or two nights.

A further problem with rocky sites (or sites in areas where the soil is shallow) is that finding effective placements for tent pegs can be extremely difficult. While this can usually be overcome by taking along a selection of different pegs, you will sometimes be forced to resort to other means of securing your tent. Pegs which have a shallow placement can often be made more secure by placing a boulder on top of them, but make sure that both the guy line and any material cannot chafe against the rock. If placing pegs turns out to be impossible, you may have to use boulders in their place, tying the guy line around them, but bear in mind the problems of chafing as outlined above (see Fig. 30).

On particularly rocky sites – where there are large boulders buried in the ground or where bedrock is exposed – it may be impossible to clear all the lumps from under the tent. In this case, notwithstanding the fact that your sleepmat will cushion you to a certain extent, you would be well advised to pad the bottom of the groundsheet with bracken, heather or some other form of vegetation or, if this is unobtainable, to place spare clothing beneath your sleeping bag.

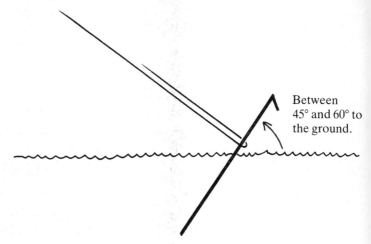

Between 45° and 60° to the ground.

**Fig. 30. Peg placement.**

SITES IN HOLLOWS

A hollow will usually give superb protection from the wind, although camping in such places can be extremely uncomfortable. Hollows can become very damp and muddy in wet weather and can also be far colder than the surrounding area due to the fact that cold air sinks and will therefore collect in them. The exceptions are shakeholes – crater-like depressions, some of which are extraordinarily large, which are often to be found in limestone areas. These are associated with cave systems, and, particularly in winter, relatively warm air from the caves below can rise up through the ground and make such depressions considerably warmer than the open land around them. However, although they offer superb shelter from the wind, finding a level site in all but the biggest shakeholes can be a problem, the drainage can often be poor and they will rarely offer you much in the way of a view!

Slight hollows can sometimes make good sites as long as they are well-drained. They may, however, be colder than their surroundings.

## WATERSIDE SITES

Sites by the side of lakes or pools can be very tempting and thoroughly enjoyable. However, such areas can be poorly drained and very cold. If you wish to camp near a pool, it is probably better (in terms of general comfort) to choose a site on a slope overlooking the water as this will inevitably be both warmer and drier. If the pool has a noticeable inflow and outflow, you would be well advised to collect your drinking and cooking water from the inflow, and do your washing and toilet by the outflow.

A further problem is that insect activity is often aggravatingly high around any body of water; an unexpected meal of human blood seems to attract midges from all over the area!

Camping by a mountain stream also has its attractions and in pleasant weather there is little to beat the sound of a bubbling brook to lull you to sleep. However, this same stream, fed by a mountain storm, can swell and become a mighty roar, banishing any hope of sleep. Worse still, the level of water in such streams can rise and fall to an alarming extent and your apparently well drained riverside site may disappear beneath the floodwaters! I once camped in unsettled weather beside a picturesque stream in the Brecon Beacons, only to have my sleep disturbed by a horrendous roar which grew in intensity as gallons of water poured into the tent!

It is worth noting that in their lower reaches (which may still be in wild country), the water level in such streams does not slowly rise, but suddenly increases in a 'flood pulse' which can have a devastating effect on a camp sited in its path. A wall of water as little as half a metre in height can do a lot of damage and flood pulses of this magnitude are not uncommon!

## WOODLAND SITES

Camping in woodlands has its attractions but can be extremely uncomfortable. It is unwise to pitch a tent directly below any trees, not least because of the danger of falling branches in high winds or thunderstorms. Moreover, although trees will give a certain amount of shelter from light showers and drizzle, if the precipitation continues for any length of time it will eventually work its way through the foliage and make its presence felt as large and noisy drops.

Root systems can often extend for a surprising distance and, even if you pitch your tent well away from any trees, you may well wake up in the middle of the night with an unsuspected and hitherto undiscovered root sticking in your side! Conversely, deep layers of fallen leaves or pine needles can act as a cushion and make your nights extremely comfortable. However, these can be damp, can attract insects and can make finding secure placements for pegs extremely difficult.

MOUNTAIN SITES

When camping high in mountainous regions, it can sometimes be difficult to find a site which fulfils all the criteria mentioned at the start of this section. In this particular situation your prime consideration should be that of shelter.

Although it is often possible to find sheltered sites in between boulders, such sites may well be both uneven and sloping. In such situations you will be forced to pad the groundsheet in some way and you will find it more comfortable if you sleep with your head facing upslope. Peg placements, too, can sometimes be difficult and you may have to resort to using boulders and tying guy lines around nearby rocks. Bear in mind the problems of chafing outlined previously.

Finally, although cliff faces and outcrops can give a high degree of shelter, it is unwise to pitch your tent directly below a large cliff, or beneath an outcrop with scree above it. Falling stones can do a lot of damage both to a tent and its occupants.

WINTER SITES

Camping in winter can be a whole different ball game, especially if the weather is unkind. Conditions can be extreme, and sub-zero temperatures combined with snow and ice can make life very uncomfortable. You would be well advised to get a reasonable amount of experience in summer conditions before setting off into the wilds in winter.

That being said, camping in wild country which is clothed in sparkling white has many attractions. As with winter walking, the mountains and moorlands seem bigger and more remote, rocks and

vegetation may be coated with exquisite ice crystals, and there is little to beat the experience of waking up to a landscape cloaked in untrodden, virgin snow.

*Winter criteria*
All the criteria which you use for choosing a camp site in summer apply just as much in winter, if not more so, and there are a number of other factors which you should take into consideration. Your water supply, for example, may be frozen, and while you may have a form of water all around you in the guise of snow and ice, this will take a long time to melt and will give a surprisingly small amount of liquid for the bulk you collected. Obtaining water in this way is a lengthy business and will use up a considerable amount of precious fuel. This should be taken into consideration when planning your trip as it will usually be necessary to take more fuel than you would in summer.

If you can find a site where there is an unfrozen spring or a supply of water beneath a frozen crust, so much the better. However, it is inadvisable to walk across the ice of frozen pools or lakes in an attempt to collect water. Apart from the fact that you run the risk of drowning if you fall through, wet clothing and winter temperatures can be a lethal mix.

While a sheltered site is of the utmost importance, you should bear in mind the problems of drifting. Snow is surprisingly heavy and if it is allowed to build up on the flysheet, it can cause the tent to collapse. This is obviously more of a problem with some tent designs than with others; those with flat roof sections are the most vulnerable.

A further problem is that drifts tend to build up on the lee side of walls, boulders and slopes, and this is exactly the position in which you will pitch your tent for maximum shelter. If you are expecting heavy snowfall or if there are high winds combined with fresh snow on the ground, it would be better for you to choose a compromise position where you get a reasonable degree of shelter without too many problems from drifting. As an added precaution, especially

Sites close to high mountain lakes can be superb, but camping right by the edge of the water is not to be recommended (see page 126).

during heavy snowfall, you can occasionally thump the inner tent against the flysheet in an attempt to dislodge any snow which may have built up.

In the same way that it is unwise to pitch your tent below a cliff face or scree slope in summer, you should beware of siting your camp below avalanche slopes or beneath cornices in winter. If you cannot recognize an avalanche slope or a cornice then, in all honesty, you should not be camping in the mountains in winter conditions!

Similarly, when camping in woodland sites, beware of snow falling from trees, particularly in a thaw. Even in cold, calm weather, the heat from your stove may cause a partial thaw directly above you and I can tell you from personal experience that there is little more frustrating than a large dollop of wet snow landing in your supper from a great height!

*Pitching on snow*
Before pitching your tent directly on to all but the most consolidated of snow, it is a good idea to stamp out an area slightly larger than the tent. If this is not done the tent may settle and the floor become uneven and uncomfortable. Stamping also makes tent peg placements more effective and long skewers or angles will usually freeze-in with surprising speed. Indeed, after a cold night, such pegs may be difficult to remove and you may have to dig them out.

In slightly warmer conditions when there is any likelihood of a thaw, you may have to secure tent pegs by placing boulders over them (if you can find any!). Here again, consolidating the snow by stamping will minimize the risk, but it may be advisable to secure the main guys on ice axes or, if the snow cover is thin, to dig down and secure pegs in the ground beneath.

Another trick worth remembering when pitching your tent is to

A comfortable camping trip in terrain and conditions such as this will require good mountaincraft as well as good campcraft. You should know the basics of safe movement on snow and ice before venturing into the mountains in these conditions.

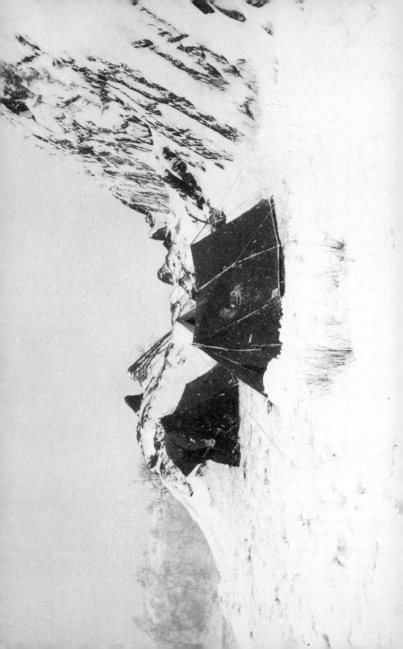

bank consolidated snow against the base of the flysheet. This will help stop any spindrift or blown snow from building up in the space between the flysheet and the inner tent. Spindrift, in particular, can be a real problem as it tends to get everywhere. Any small gap left between the ends of the door zips is particularly vulnerable for you can guarantee that the spindrift will find its way through this and into the inner tent. Try to minimize this by blocking the gap with something and get rid of any spindrift that collects in the doorway at regular intervals.

## 2.5   Camp routine

The term 'routine' has been mentioned a number of times in previous sections with reference to various aspects of camp life. Camp routines will vary not only from person to person but also, to a certain degree, from site to site and from season to season. However, many parts of the routine will remain similar, whatever the circumstances.

I must emphasize that, as with everything else in this part of the book, the following description is not a set of hard and fast rules but a series of suggestions based purely on personal preference and experience. Those of you who have already had some experience of wild country camping may well have a routine which is totally different to mine, although I imagine that there will be several similarities.

As mentioned previously, there can be no doubt that some form of routine can go a long way towards making camp life that little bit more comfortable. This is particularly true when things are not running smoothly owing to unkind weather conditions or any number of other factors. After a modicum of experience, you will probably find that your routine becomes habituated and you will do certain things almost without thinking.

Perhaps one of the easiest ways to illustrate a camp routine is to look at a typical sequence of events, taking us from arrival at the site to departure.

A well-sheltered winter site.

ARRIVAL
Unless the weather is horrific, in which case you will probably want
to get your tent up as soon as possible, dump your gear, get out your
stove and make a brew. Apart from being a superb morale booster,
this will give you time to get the feel of the site and to select the best
position for your tent. If the weather is cold or windy, but not overly
wet, you can always pitch your tent while the water is heating.

Once you have decided upon a position, clear an area of ground,
slightly larger than the floor of the tent, of any loose stones or other
objects which might damage the groundsheet or cause discomfort
when you lie down. Once this has been done you are ready to pitch
your tent.

Although different tents are pitched in different ways, generally
speaking you should peg out the groundsheet first, making sure that
the edges are straight and reasonably taut. Carry on pitching
according to the manufacturer's instructions, making sure that pole
sections are correctly inserted and that any pull from pegs or from
guy lines runs in line with the seams. On some tents it is possible to
use the same peg for both inner tent peg points and the
corresponding flysheet peg points. If this is done you must be
careful that the separation between the inner and flysheet is not
affected. Whatever method you use, try to insert the pegs at an
angle of between 60° and 45° away from the direction of strain (Fig.
31). Once pitched, make sure that the tent is stable, that there are
no undue stresses and that the fabric is reasonably taut. If any
adjustments are necessary, it is far easier to make them now than to
get up in the middle of the night, especially if the weather has taken
a turn for the worse.

When you are satisfied with the tent, unpack your rucksack of all
the gear that will be needed during the coming hours, take your
sleeping bag from its stuff sack, give it a good shake and lay it out
ready so that it can breathe. If the weather is suitable, you can air
your sleeping bag for a short while by laying it over the flysheet.
When you come to put it (or anything else) in the tent, remember to
take off your boots first or, at the very least, lie or kneel in the
entrance of the tent so that the boots are outside.

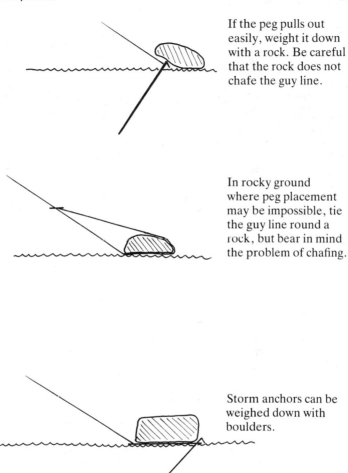

If the peg pulls out easily, weight it down with a rock. Be careful that the rock does not chafe the guy line.

In rocky ground where peg placement may be impossible, tie the guy line round a rock, but bear in mind the problem of chafing.

Storm anchors can be weighed down with boulders.

**Fig. 31. Peg placements in difficult situations.**

*Above*: Pitching camp (1). The A-frame of a mountain ridge tent provides a very stable supporting structure. Note that the groundsheet has been roughly pegged-out. *Below*: Pitching camp (2). Final adjustments are made to both the poles and the groundsheet once the inner is attached to the frame.

*Above*: Pitching camp (3). Battling with the flysheet! No matter what model tent you use, a high wind will create problems. *Below*: Pitching camp (4). The tent finally erected. Note the use of side guy lines to maintain the separation between the flysheet and the inner tent.

## WET WEATHER

The golden rule in wet weather is to keep wet gear out of the tent. Obviously, this is easier to do if you have space under the flysheet in which to store equipment and wet clothing. Some form of porch extension or flysheet bell-end by the entrance is also invaluable as this means you can take off your waterproofs and boots whilst under cover but not inside the inner tent.

However careful you are, there is always the possibility that a small amount of moisture may get into the tent. If this happens, mop it up immediately or it will spread like wildfire. A small sponge (mentioned in Section 1.5) will be very useful in this respect.

If the weather is so bad that you need to cook in the tent, it is advisable to fold your sleeping bag in half and place it at the back of the tent along with any items not stored under the flysheet. Make sure that everything is well out of harm's way and in such a position that it is not going to get wet, catch fire or become covered in any spilled food.

Generally speaking, if the weather or ground is at all wet, you should try to keep movement in and out of the tent to a minimum. The more times you enter the tent, the more the chance of getting things wet.

## WINTER CONDITIONS

If there is snow on the ground you should consolidate an area slightly larger than the tent before pitching. It will also be advisable to bank snow against the base of the flysheet in order to minimize the problem of snow and spindrift filling the gap between the flysheet and inner tent.

Get into the habit of brushing snow from your clothing before getting into the tent and keep movement in and out of the tent to a minimum, especially if it is windy and there is fresh snow falling or on the ground. Spindrift, in particular, can be a big problem as it seems seek out any little gap or hole; I have even known it pour into a tent through the ventilation mesh! Although it can be difficult and, at times, will seem well nigh impossible, you must do your utmost to prevent as much spindrift as possible from finding its way into the inner tent. Plug holes and gaps with anything which will not be damaged or which does not matter if it becomes wet, and clear away the spindrift which does manage to find its way in at regular intervals.

If it is snowing heavily or if there is any drifting taking place, try not to leave small items lying on the ground as they may soon become covered. Additionally, it will be advisable to brush off any snow which sticks to the flysheet at fairly regular intervals. Apart from the fact that it can destroy that all important separation between flysheet and inner tent, snow (especially wet snow which sticks very easily) is remarkably heavy and can build up to such an extent that it may cause your tent to collapse.

COOKING

The most common form of camping injuries are burns and scalds. It is therefore of the utmost importance that you are safety-conscious when cooking, especially when conditions have forced you to cook inside your tent. Generally speaking you will find it easier to appoint someone to do the cooking, then leave them to get on with it. If you are alone, the problem does not arise and if there are only two or three of you, you can take it in turns. If you are a member of a large group with two or more tents, it may be found more convenient for each tent to be self-contained in terms of cooking.

First and foremost, it is good practice to prepare a cooking area. This does not have to be anything spectacular but it should contain a steady, stable and solid base for your stove. Particularly when cooking outside, it will help if there is also some form of shelter from the wind and this can be achieved by cooking in amongst boulders, in a slight hollow, or by constructing a windbreak out of any available materials.

If the weather is bad you may be forced to cook under shelter. If your tent is suitable, this is best done in the entrance under cover of the flysheet. With tents that have no suitable space you will have to cook in the tent, in which case you should site your stove as near the entrance as practicable. Make sure the stove is stable, preferably sitting on a non-inflammable surface (i.e. a slab of rock or the lid of a billycan). If possible, cook alone. Any companions can either don waterproofs and sit it out outside, or wait with rumbling stomachs in

A paraffin pressure stove in use. Note how the stove is on a firm base in a
sheltered position, with a windshield around the burner. You should hold
the pan whenever you stir the contents or adjust the flame.

another tent. If there is no other tent and if conditions are such that
it is preferable for them to be under shelter, make sure that anyone
with you stays well out of the way towards the rear of the tent.

Whatever the weather and wherever you cook, it will save much
time and effort if you lay out everything to hand before you start
cooking. Try to plan things so that you can cook the complete meal
without having to relight the stove. You can always eat one course
whilst the next is cooking. Use lids to conserve heat (and therefore
fuel) whenever possible, and always hold the pan when you add to
or stir the ingredients or adjust the flame. Things like quick-cook
rice and pasta can be heated on the stove and then left in a covered

pan to cook in their own heat while you continue to cook the other ingredients. Pans can also be 'stacked' (i.e. placed on top of one another), but in this case it is essential that the stove is on a very firm base as the whole structure is inherently unstable.

When taking pans off the stove and placing them on the ground, make sure that they go on to a level surface. If cooking inside the tent, it is inadvisable to place hot pans directly on to the groundsheet unless you want neat round holes melted! Mugs, in particular, have a nasty habit of falling over – one way round this is to place them inside boots. This also provides insulation and will keep the drink warm for slightly longer than would otherwise be the case.

Always boil more water than you think you will need; there is nothing quite so frustrating as being unable to complete cooking a meal until fresh water has been boiled. Any excess water can be used in brews or to do the washing-up. With regard to the latter it makes life far easier if you soak the pans immediately you have finished with them. It is also a good idea to get into the habit of washing-up as soon as the meal is over – cold grease can be unbelievably stubborn and it is not a good start to the day if you have to spend time scrubbing a dirty pan before you can cook breakfast. However, if food has been burnt to the extent that the pan is blackened and coated with a hard mess, it will probably be less frustrating to soak it in water overnight. Adding a little salt will also help. Some people take a small quantity of washing-up liquid with them but I find this unnecessary, especially if you take a soap-filled scouring pad.

EVENINGS
Lying back on the ground, watching the sunset and relaxing after a hard day, is one of the joys of camping in wild country. However, the weather will not always be kind enough, and there are often a number of chores which need to be done. There may be mending to do and gear to sort out; you may want to plan a route or prepare for the following day's activities.

If you are staying at the same site for any length of time you should consider digging some form of latrine. This does not have to

Putting your mug inside a boot not only keeps the contents warm, but also means it is less likely to be knocked over accidentally.

be anything spectacular – just a small hole in the ground, preferably in a reasonably sheltered and possibly hidden position a short distance from the tents (see also Section 2.6 and Fig. 32). In any event, faeces should be buried not less than 15 centimetres deep, and used toilet paper should be burnt and the ash buried with the faeces.

As has already been noted, general hygiene is important. It is, for example, advisable to wash your hands before cooking or eating. Foot hygiene, in particular, should be regarded as essential. Take the opportunity in the evenings to attend to any 'hot spots' (i.e. the sore area before a blister fills with liquid) or minor blisters, and keep your feet clean. Although it is arguably better to wear dirty

Not less than 30 cm deep.

End on view. Note soil piled to one side.

Turfs stacked to one end.

View from above. Note saved turfs. The length of the trench will depend on the length of your stay!

**Fig. 32. A simple latrine.**

socks than wet ones, given suitable weather many people wash their socks in the evenings, leaving them to dry over a guy line, a nearby rock or branch, or a length of paracord rigged up as a washing-line. However, washing in the evenings can pose problems, for when the weather is settled and the sky clear (conditions which are apparently ideal for washing and overnight drying), there may well be a heavy dew. For this reason some people do any necessary washing in the morning, and you may find this more convenient, even if you have to strap wet clothing on to a rucksack to dry as you walk along. That being said, you can often usefully air damp clothing in the early evening.

Some people like to keep diaries or logs, and these are better filled in each evening when things are fresh in the mind, rather than waiting until your return when you may have forgotten a thing or two. Others like to take a good book or, in good weather, to go for a leisurely stroll at dusk. However, whatever your preferences, unless you are camping alone you will find that evening conversation is one of the most pleasant parts of the camping experience. Because of the nature of the surroundings, there is usually little room for phoney pretentions or putting on an act, and conversation almost inevitably becomes philosophical in nature. Friendships made around a purring pressure stove often stand the test of time!

If there are any problems with midges or other biting animals, it is generally during the evenings that these will make their presence felt with a vengeance. This is when you will be pleased that you brought along some insect repellent. What you should try to do is stop any insect getting underneath your clothing. As such it is best to use the repellent around your neck, wrists and ankles. If you wear breeches and stockings, don't forget that midges can find their way through the wool. In such circumstances it will be useful to apply repellent to your shins and calves.

As mentioned earlier, mosquito coils can be useful to prevent insects getting inside the tent where they can have a good overnight meal. Another way to reduce the likelihood of unwelcome visitors inside the tent is to place insect repellent liberally over the tent door.

TURNING IN

During the long cold nights of winter, when darkness falls with astonishing speed and sometimes unexpectedly early, you will often find that you settle down for the night at times which, in the civilized world, would still be full of activity. Even so, many people will don their head-torch and read for a couple of hours, cosy in their sleeping bag, or light a candle and talk about hopes and dreams (or nothing in particular) for hours on end. Whatever the season, whatever the time, it is not a bad idea to have a light supper or, at the very least, a hot brew before turning in.

Some people like to get their breakfast sorted out before going to bed so that it is all easily to hand the following morning. I know one hedonistic soul who, in cold conditions, heats very much more than enough water for his evening brew, putting the remainder back in his aluminium water-bottle and taking it to bed with him! Although the thought of a hot water-bottle may run contrary to some people's spartan ideal, in particularly cold weather it is not a bad idea to put your water-bottle in your sleeping bag with you. At the very least it lessens the likelihood that it will be frozen in the morning. If your boots are wet, you can place these inside a plastic bag and put them in your sleeping bag as well!

Again in cold weather, it is useful to have your stove, a pan and all the necessary ingredients for a brew close to hand, either in the tent or within easy reach outside the door, under the flysheet. If you wake in the chilly, early hours of a winter's morning you may be glad of the chance to lie back in the warmth of your sleeping bag while water is heating for a brew. However, if you do this, beware the problems of poor ventilation and condensation, and remember that it is unwise to store gas stoves or their cartridges inside the tent (see Section 1.4).

If having a stove close to hand is useful, so too is a torch, not least because it will make those inconvenient middle-of-the-night calls of nature slightly less unpleasant! During extremely cold temperatures at higher altitudes, where the thought of donning boots and duvet and staggering into the deep-freeze conditions outside is just that little bit too much, you may wish to use a pee-bottle. Better this than fumbling around in the entrance of the tent with all its attendant and fairly obvious hazards!

## BREAKFAST

If the weather is cold and you are using gas as a cooking fuel, your first task on waking should be to put your stove (or the cartridge you intend to use) inside your sleeping bag. As has been noted, gas and cold weather are not a particularly good combination, and placing the fuel inside a warm sleeping bag will go a long way towards making your breakfast a less frustrating meal to cook.

It is not a bad idea to open the tent door as quietly as possible, because you never know what you are going to see. During a particularly memorable camp in the wilds of mid-Wales, I quietly poked my head out of the tent one morning to find a red kite perched on a tree not more than a couple of metres away. If the weather is good, grab your sleeping bag and air it over the tent or, if the tent is wet with dew, over a line rigged from paracord or something similar. As soon as any condensation has disappeared from the outside shell, turn it inside out and air the inside. Any damp clothing can be aired at the same time.

Breakfast should be a leisurely affair, and all the factors which have been mentioned in terms of cooking safety should be borne in mind, especially if, like me, you take a long time to wake up and tend to fumble around for a while. Most people start by boiling water which can be used for that all important brew as well as for cereals (in combination with dried milk). While eating your bacon and eggs (or whatever else you have) boil some more water for use in flasks or for the washing-up. Odd tasks such as getting day snacks ready, washing socks or simply perusing guidebooks and maps can be done while your digestive system is getting to work on your food.

## STRIKING CAMP

Striking camp in wet weather can be a nightmare. You will want to do as much as possible under cover, so the tent (or one of the tents if there are a few of you) should be left until last. Packing a rucksack in the confines of a small tent is not an easy task but it is better to persevere than to wander outside and get everything soaked. In this instance you should pack one at a time, with the other people staying out of the tent to leave more room. However, if the rain seems to be in the form of a passing shower, it is probably better to wait until it has passed, although such passing showers often have a nasty habit of merging into one another and the ground will obviously be wet.

Whatever the conditions, try to ensure that as much as possible is clean and dry, even if you have to spend a little time cleaning it. If it is necessary to pack wet or dirty items inside the main body of the rucksack, it is advisable to put them in plastic bags.

Particularly if you are continuing to another camp, it is of vital importance that you ensure you have *everything* with you. When packing the stove, for example, make sure that all the necessary parts are there. If not, find them and pack them in their proper place. It is of little good assuming that a missing part will come to light at the next site simply because it has been packed elsewhere or has been taken by someone else because, in all probability, it will not.

Pack your rucksack in the same order and in the same way as it was packed at the beginning of the trip. If you get into the habit of packing your rucksack in a particular way you should quickly become aware if any items are missing.

Once you are packed and ready to go, have a good look round the area to make sure that nothing has been left and that nothing seems out of place. If, for example, you have dug a latrine, fill it in and replace any turf. All rubbish should be removed from the site, with the possible exception of paper and card which can be burnt and the resulting ash buried at least 20 centimetres deep. Nothing should be left – if you carried it in you can carry it out. Within a few days there should be nothing to indicate that you have been there.

## 2.6   Extended trips

Although the vast majority of people who go camping in wild country will seldom stay away for more than two or three days at a time, many devotees may like the idea of longer trips to more remote areas, possibly even to one of the vast wilderness areas found in other parts of the world. While the intricacies of expedition planning lie way beyond the scope of this book, it may be helpful to look at some of the extra factors which should be borne in mind when planning and preparing for the more lengthy trips.

There are basically two types of extended trip: those in which you are constantly mobile, moving camp fairly regularly, and those in which your camp is used as a base for a specific activity. Of the two, the mobile camp is by far the more common and such trips are often undertaken in this country by people following long-distance footpaths or backpacking their way across Scotland.

Assuming that you can visit some form of settlement every two or three days in order to stock up on food, fuel and any other essential supplies, there is little difference between this type of extended trip and the more usual two or three nights away. However, it would be wise to check that such things as stove fuel and suitable foodstuffs are readily available from local suppliers because, except in the more popular areas, small village shops rarely stock gas cartridges and dehydrated ration packs. You might also like to think carefully about clothing. Items which are light and low in bulk, easy to wash and quick-drying will have considerable advantages over some of the more traditional garments.

Long trips using static camps are a totally different proposition, especialy if the base camps are situated miles away from the nearest habitation. In addition to everything discussed so far, you will need to think very carefully about a number of other factors.

FOOD AND FUEL

One of the biggest problems with living in a remote base camp is that of supplies. If you are away for any length of time, it is going to be virtually impossible for you to carry sufficient food and fuel with you and you will have to resort to one of a number of alternatives. Depending on the size of the party and the geographical location of the camp, it may be possible to send one or more people to the nearest habitation at reasonably regular intervals, simply to keep your supplies topped up. The alternative is to take sufficient supplies from the outset, carried either by persons not staying for the full duration of the camp or possibly by hired help of some description.

Whatever method is chosen, it is important that you do a certain amount of basic research before going on such a trip. For example, planning each meal in advance means that you will get a better idea of the quantities of food and fuel needed. When estimating fuel quantities, remember to take into account not only meals but also the occasional brew – of which there may be a fair quantity.

You may also like to consider taking along some form of flysheet extension or perhaps even an extra tent. This can be used not only as a store for gear, foodstuffs, etc., but also as a 'kitchen'. It may also have several other uses, as we will see later.

A flysheet extension can be useful on extended trips.

## WASHING AND DRYING

Although I am not suggesting that you need to set up a mobile launderette, on any extended trip there will doubtless be a certain amount of washing that you wish to do, even if this only comprises socks and shirts. There is little need to take along washing-powders as biodegradable soap can be used both for personal hygiene and washing clothes. It should also be fairly simple to rig up some form of washing-line.

Furthermore, if the weather is inclement, you may be faced with a fair amount of wet clothing. In order to let wet gear start to dry under cover, you can rig up a line slung between the poles of a flysheet extension. Semi-dry gear can then be given a final airing outside, if and when the weather improves.

In fine, sunny weather, draping damp gear over warm (but clean) rocks is very effective.

## GENERAL HYGIENE

During an extended stay at one site it will be necessary to dig some form of latrine. In its most simple form this is a narrow trench about half a metre deep, the soil from which is piled to one side and the turf removed and kept. The length of the trench will depend upon both the length of stay and the number of people at the camp. After each use, the toilet paper is burnt and the resulting ashes and faeces are covered with soil. Finally, before leaving the site, the trench is refilled and the turfs are replaced. There should be no visible signs of the latrine when you leave the area.

You may also like to dig a grease pit into which you can pour washing up water, waste food, etc. This need not be anything spectacular – a simple hole in the ground is quite sufficient. As with your latrine, remove any turf first, keep this to one side and replace it again on departure.

Minor cuts and abrasions, hot spots and blisters, and all forms of minor injuries should be treated as soon as possible. Antiseptic creams or lotions should therefore form an essential part of the first aid equipment carried. Foot care is especially important during trips where a fair degree of walking is involved. Both feet and socks should be washed regularly and toe-nails should kept short and cut straight.

Camping lanterns: gas (left) and petrol pressure.

It is wise to ensure that your hands are clean before preparing or eating food. As has already been mentioned, a minor stomach upset which might be regarded as a slight nuisance in more civilized areas can lead to several problems during extended camps. Apart from any other considerations, it will usually leave you feeling weak and lethargic, and may make you more prone to other complaints.

## LIGHTING
Although you may well have head-torches and candles, during extended trips it will often be found useful to take some slightly more efficient form of lighting with you, this usually taking the form of a lantern of some description.

The most convenient types of lanterns are those powered by gas. You simple turn them on and light them, and many models have some form of automatic ignition. The alternative is to take a hurricane-lantern of some description, powered either by petrol or, more commonly, by paraffin. The advantages and disadvantages of the different types of fuel have already been mentioned in Section 1.4 and, generally speaking, the things which apply to stoves apply equally to lanterns.

If you decide to carry a lantern, it would be wise to take some spare mantles as well, as these tend to be fairly fragile. You should also remember to take along spare batteries for head-torches or hand-held torches.

ADDITIONAL EQUIPMENT
Many people will wish to take along a few extra items in order to make camp life more comfortable. In addition to the few items mentioned above, you may like to consider taking soft shoes for use when in the tent, and digging latrines and grease pits will be easier if you have an entrenching tool of some description.

If you want to receive regular weather forecasts, the easiest method is via a small radio. If you have a radio included in a personal stereo, so much the better, as you can take along your favourite cassettes to make the occasional long night or storm-bound day less tedious. In these situations, a good book or two can be worth the extra weight, such books and cassettes often finding their way around the entire camp. I have discovered several new authors and pieces of music in this way!

LITTER
Anyone who has visited base camp areas in the major mountain regions of the world cannot fail to be sickened by the amount of rubbish, litter and discarded gear left lying around. Whilst one can, perhaps, appreciate the practical difficulties posed by the removal of such litter, there can nowadays be no excuse whatsoever for leaving a site in a disgusting state. No matter how long you stay at your site, within a few days of your departure it should be impossible to tell that someone has been there.

Flammable litter (i.e. cardboard cartons, paper, wood, unwanted clothing, etc.) should be burnt and the resulting ashes buried. Biodegradable litter (i.e. waste food) should be buried after having been burnt if possible. In very remote areas used regularly as a base camp, it may arguably be permissible (and thoughtful) to leave any non-perishable foodstuffs (i.e. tins) that you do not wish to carry out, but in this case they should be made into an obvious cache and covered with stones.

Abandonment of gear high on a mountain may be necessary for a number of reasons but there are few situations in which this is necessary at a base camp. Quite simply, if you packed it in you can pack it out, even if you then discard it properly at a later stage.

**Part Three**

# Appendices

**Appendix I: Wild country in Britain** (see Fig. 33)
Compared with many other parts of the world, wild country in
Britain is becoming increasingly rare. However, the odd pockets
that still remain each have a character all of their own and it is this
incredible variety of scenery within a relatively small area which
gives the British Isles their attraction for many people.

With certain exceptions, most of the wild country in England and
Wales is included in one of the ten National Parks, the major
exception being mid-Wales. Each area is described below. While
there are no National Parks in Scotland, there are five regions
covered by National Park Direction Area Orders, a number of
Forest Parks set up by the Forestry Commission, and fifteen
National Scenic Areas, some of which lie in very remote
countryside.

THE NATIONAL PARKS

1. *Brecon Beacons (Parc Cenedlaethol Bannau Brycheiniog)*
This is an upland area of over 1300 square kilometres, consisting
predominantly of flat-topped mountains and wild moorland cut by
lush valleys. There are several distinct areas including the Black
Mountains to the east, the central massif of the Brecon Beacons
themselves and, somewhat confusingly, the Black Mountain to the
west. A limestone belt along the southern boundary is noted for its
extensive cave systems, and south of the central area is the
Waterfall Country, a dramatic area of steep-sided, wooded valleys
and gorges with superb waterfalls and torrents.

Information centres can be found at Abergavenny, Brecon and
Llandovery.

1. Loch Torridon
2. Glen Affric
3. Cairngorms
4. Ben Nevis
5. Trossachs
6. Northumberland National Park
7. Lake District National Park
8. Yorkshire Dales National Park
9. North York Moors National Park
10. Peak District National Park
11. Snowdonia National Park
12. Mid-Wales
13. Pembrokeshire Coast National Park
14. Brecon Beacons National Park
15. Dartmoor National Park
16. Exmoor National Park

**Fig. 33. Wild country in Britain.**

## 2. *Dartmoor*

This is rightly regarded as the last great wilderness of southern Britain, covering an area of over 900 square kilometres. Extremely wild (and boggy) in places, there may be access problems in the northern sector due to military training. Famous for its tors and quaking bogs, the area also contains some fine gorges and river valleys.

Information centres can be found at Exeter, Newton Abbot, Okehampton and Plymouth.

## 3. *Exmoor*

The smallest of the English National Parks, covering an area of under 700 square kilometres, the region is predominantly one of high heather moorland cut by deep combes. The northern boundary runs along the coast of the Bristol Channel. Although the moorland supports herds of red deer, the area is increasingly under threat from intensive agriculture. Indeed, the heather moors which the park was supposed to conserve have shrunk from 25,000 hectares to under 16,000 hectares.

Information centres can be found at Combe Martin, Minehead, Lynmouth and Lynton.

## 4. *Lake District*

At just under 2300 square kilometres, this is the largest of the National Parks covering a superb and unique landscape of high fells and picturesque lakes and tarns. Although under threat from both water authorities and its own popularity, it is still possible to get away from the crowds and find some delightfully isolated areas.

Information centres can be found at Ambleside, Broughton in Furness and Keswick.

## 5. *Northumberland*

An area of about 1000 square kilometres of lonely, rolling hills, including the superbly bleak Cheviots and the heathlands of the Simonside Hills. To the north, the area is affected by the MoD's Redesdale Training Area, and the whole region is fast becoming choked by a horrendous blanket of conifers.

Information centres can be found at Hexham, Newcastle-upon-Tyne, Otterburn and Rothbury.

## 6. *North York Moors*
Including the largest area of heather moor south of Scotland, this National Park contains just over 1400 square kilometres of delightful and varied scenery. Surrounding the flat-topped Cleveland Hills are the superb, rolling limestone dales, and to the east is a rugged coastal area.

Information centres can be found at Middlesbrough, Northallerton, Saltburn and Whitby.

## 7. *Peak District*
This, the first of the ten National Parks to be designated, covers an area of some 1400 square kilometres which can be split into two distinct regions. The 'Dark Peak' covers the peaty moors and gritstone edges to the north, while the 'White Peak' covers the spectacular limestone dales to the south. It is both the most popular and populous of the National Parks.

Information centres can be found at Ashbourne, Bakewell, Buxton, Manchester and Sheffield.

## 8. *Pembrokeshire coast* (Parc Cenedlaethol Penfro)
The smallest of all the National Parks, this region of just under 600 square kilometres contains over 270 kilometres of some of the most dramatic coastal scenery in Europe. The mysterious and atmospheric Prescelli Hills are also included in the area. Although spoilt to a certain extent by caravan sites and chalet developments, and playing host to the tanks of NATO countries who come to play on the Castlemartin ranges, this is none the less an incomparable area, although it offers little scope for really wild camping.

Information centres can be found at Fishguard, Milford Haven, Pembroke, St David's and Tenby.

## 9. *Snowdonia* (Parc Cenedlaethol Eryri)
The largest Welsh National Park (and, at just over 2100 square kilometres, second only to the Lake District), this area offers plenty

of scope for wild country camping. The scenery is amazingly varied, stretching from the rocky peaks and wild mountains of central Snowdonia and Cadair Idris to delightful wooded valleys, coastal dunes and muddy estuaries.

Information centres can be found at Bangor, Caernarfon, Conway and Machynlleth.

## 10. *Yorkshire Dales*
Comprising over 1750 square kilometres of high, open fells and superbly green dales, there is a wealth of scenery here for all to enjoy. Pockmarked by caves and pot-holes, this superb area is also threatened by quarrying and forestry but still offers plenty of scope for those who want to get away from it all.

Information centres can be found at Harrogate, Ilkley, Skipton and Richmond.

### MID-WALES
The area lying between the Brecon Beacons and Snowdonia has all the qualities of scenic beauty and isolation which most people associate with National Parks. Surprisingly remote, dotted with isolated farms, the vast upland areas are criss-crossed by superb river valleys and wooded gorges, many of which are becoming popular tourist attractions. Although there are access problems in some areas, there is still ample scope for wild country camping. Indeed, it is possible to find places here that feel (and are) far more remote than in many of the National Parks.

### SCOTLAND
There are no National Parks in Scotland, mainly because so much area could be designated that it would make a mockery of the system. Once you are away from the centres of population and industry, there are vast areas of wilderness. Although, traditionally, access to the hills has never been a problem, there have recently been problems associated with large consortia buying old estates and using them for profits from deer-stalking, grouse-shooting, game-fishing, etc. So long as you bear in mind the various game seasons, generally speaking you will have few problems.

In many ways it seems invidious to single out any particular area as being better than others. However, I have to say that my favourite areas include the magnificent Cairngorms and the North-West Highlands and Islands.

NATIONAL PARK DIRECTION AREA ORDERS
There are five Scottish regions covered by the above designation, which together make up only about 6% of the total area – a minuscule amount when compared with the whole. These regions are Ben Nevis, Glen Coe and Black Mount (just under 1600 square kilometres of the Western Highlands and moorlands); the Cairngorms (just under 500 square kilometres of some of the most remote and spectacular mountain scenery in Britain); Glen Affric, Glen Cannich and Strathfarrar (just under 700 square kilometres of the wild highlands to be found to the north-west of the Caledonian Canal); Loch Lomond and the Trossachs (just over 800 square kilometres of superb moorland and highland swimming with idyllic lochs); and Loch Torridon, Loch Marie and Loch Broom (over 2000 square kilometres of the incomparable north-west highland region).

As well as these, there are fifteen areas which have been designated as National Scenic Areas. These include several remote lochs, the Black Cuillins of Skye, and many of the beautiful islands to be found along the western coast. Indeed, the coastal areas of the north-west are well worth a visit. Almost the total length has been designated as a coastal conservation zone, and often has excellent weather due to the proximity of the Gulf Stream. Further details, if required, can be obtained from the relevant Tourist Boards.


## Appendix II: The legal position
In the most simple terms, there is only one rule that should be taken into consideration whenever or wherever you go camping: because all land is owned by someone, you must get the permission of the landowner before camping on his land. This applies as much to areas of land designated as National Parks as it does to any other area.

The term 'National Park' does not necessarily mean that there are any special rights of access to that part of the countryside. Indeed, most areas within National Parks are still in private ownership. Even when this is not so, when National Park Authorities have purchased areas of land, there may well be local by-laws or similar conditions which prohibit camping.

That being said, if you are planning to camp at a remote site in wild country, it may be well nigh impossible to contact the landowner, let alone get written permission to camp. Many large estates, conservation bodies and investment companies which hold areas of land are loath to give any such permission because, in doing so, they may become legally liable if you suffer an injury whilst camping on land in their control. As it happens, under the common law duty of care, they may be liable anyway, even if you are trespassing! Additionally, tracing landowners can be a long and tedious job, and even if you do trace the landowner, many areas of land are owned by large consortia or held in trust, and finding the right person to contact is not easy. Getting a reply is also sometimes extremely difficult.

In practice, so long as you camp on the high fells or open moorland, well away from any areas of enclosed farmland and outside any specially designated areas of land such as National Nature Reserves or Sites of Special Scientific Interest, there will rarely be any problem. Although it is no legal defence, the phrase 'out of sight, out of mind' has a particular relevance here. However, certain landowners guard their land more jealously than others, particularly when such land is used for grouse-shooting or deer-stalking, and it is always a good idea to enquire in the locality or to seek advice from locals or, where applicable, from National Park wardens.

If you are camping anywhere without permission and are asked to leave, you should do so politely and without complaint. A landowner is perfectly within his rights to eject you from his land, so long as he only uses 'reasonable force'! The farmer who threatens you with a shotgun or sets his dogs on you (both very rare occurrences but they have happened) is himself committing an offence, although that is of little comfort when it happens!

## TRESPASS

Contrary to popular belief, trespass is not a criminal offence but a civil one. The sign 'Trespassers will be Prosecuted' is normally no more than 'a wooden falsehood'. Such signs would be more correct if they said 'Trespassers will be Sued', the landowner suing the trespasser for damages. Arriving at a figure for damages would not be an easy task unless, of course, the trespasser had caused damage to crops, livestock, buildings, etc.

However, the entry on to another's land is legally wrong whether or not the entrant knows that he is trespassing. It is no defence that the only reason for entry was that he had lost his way, or even that he genuinely or erroneously believed that he had the right of entry.

There are a number of different types of trespass. The one of most interest in our context is trespass to land. Trespass to land is purely and simply the possession or occupation, even for a short period of time, of land belonging to another. The only defences which may be of use are that of licence (i.e. the landowner has given his permission) and that of justification by law (i.e. the right to use public footpaths, any right granted by the Countryside Acts, etc.). Although there are certain areas of land where there is *de facto* access for walking, this will rarely be the case for camping.

If you are found trespassing or camping without permission, the owner has the right to eject you from his land. He can also sue you for any damage done, can take out a court injunction forbidding you to re-enter his land, and may be able to bring an action for mesne profits which is a form of charge for occupation!

## WILDLIFE AND COUNTRYSIDE ACT 1981

Whilst many parts of this Act are of no direct relevance to camping in wild country, Part One of the Act deals with the preservation of various species of birds and animals, and Part Two deals with the protection of certain areas of land. It is a criminal offence to do damage to areas protected under this Act, and if, for example, you were camping in such an area and in doing so you destroyed a protected plant, you could be prosecuted. This would apply particularly in areas such as National Nature Reserves and Sites of

Special Scientific Interest where camping is usually strictly
forbidden. There may well be local by-laws in other areas
(particularly areas of common ground) which prohibit camping.

Although there are usually few problems associated with
considerate overnight camping in remote areas, you would be well
advised to bear the above points in mind. If you intend to camp
regularly, you might like to visit your local Citizens Advice Bureau
or a solicitor for further information on the ramifications of the laws
of trespass and the ways in which the Wildlife and Countryside Acts
may have a bearing on your chosen activities. If visiting a National
Park, it will do no harm to write to the Information Officer and ask
his advice.

## Appendix III: The country and mountain codes

THE COUNTRY CODE
*Guard against all risk of fire*
If you decide to have a camp fire, make sure that you remove the
underlying turf and ensure that there is no danger to surrounding
vegetation. Heaths, plantations, woodlands and fellsides can all be
highly inflammable. Make sure any fires are totally extinguished
before departure, and replace the removed turfs.
   If you discover a fire, try to stamp it out. If it is too big for you or
others to deal with, report the blaze as quickly as possible to the fire
brigade, police or Forestry Commission officers.

*Leave all gates as you find them*
If you are walking along a public right of way, any gate should
either be unlocked or there should be a stile nearby. If there is no
stile and the gate is unlocked, open and close it as opposed to
climbing it, making sure that it is securely closed behind you. If the
gate is open when you arrive, leave it open. If, for some reason, you
have to climb over a gate, climb it at the hinge end.

*Keep dogs under proper control*
Generally speaking, you should keep any dog on a lead whenever there is livestock around, and when you are walking along narrow country roads.

*Keep to paths across farmland*
When crossing areas of enclosed farmland, follow footpaths carefully. When travelling from valley areas to the open mountain, be careful to find the correct paths.

Recognized or legal routes are usually signposted in some way, either by the standard 'Public Footpath' or 'Public Bridleway' signs, by patches of coloured paint, by a figure of a walking man, or perhaps by cairns. Long Distance Footpaths are usually waymarked by an 'acorn'. Always use the gates and stiles provided on such routes, even if the path detours to reach them.

*Avoid damaging fences, hedges and walls*
There should be no reason for you to cross a wall, fence or hedge by any other means than a stile or gate if you are on a public footpath. However, some paths become obstructed, so if you are forced to cross such obstructions, do so carefully causing no damage.

When on the open mountain, cross dry stone walls via the nearest gate or stile, or detour until you reach a point where you can cross with ease and without risk of causing damage.

*Leave no litter*
Take *all* your litter home with you. There is no excuse for leaving anything behind. Leave the countryside as you would wish to find it. Do not bury litter – animals may dig it up again, and remember that opened tins, plastic bags and broken glass can be fatal to both domestic and wild animals.

*Safeguard water supplies*
Many farms and isolated rural communities rely directly on springs as their sole source of drinking water. Do not build dams or pollute the water in any way. Similarly, do not pollute cattle-troughs or any other form of water storage or water supply.

*Protect wildlife, wild plants and trees*
The countryside is best seen, not collected. Do not pick wild
flowers, disturb wild animals or birds, carve your initials on trees or
leave graffiti of any description.

Many plants and animals are now protected by law. It is a
criminal offence to pick certain wild flowers and to disturb many
species of animals and birds.

*Go carefully on country roads*
Country roads are usually narrow and winding, often with high
banks or hedges on either side. When travelling by vehicle, drive
slowly and carefully, and be considerate to other road users. Slow to
a crawl if you meet people on horseback. If the road is narrow, stop,
and let the horses pass you. Do not rev the engine nor sound the
horn.

When walking along country roads, keep to the right and listen
for oncoming traffic. Often you will hear a vehicle long before the
driver can see you. At sharp bends on roads with high banks or
hedges, it may be better to walk on the outside of the bend, even if
this means you cross to the left side of the road.

*Respect the life of the countryside*
Many people live and work in the country. Respect the property,
livelihood and privacy of local residents.

THE MOUNTAIN CODE

*Be prepared*
Make sure you are properly clothed and equipped for the proposed
journey and the possible weather conditions. Seek advice if you are
unsure of the correct gear. Equipment is of little use unless it is
sound and you know how to use it correctly. You should have a
reasonable knowledge of basic first aid, and good knowledge and
experience of mountaincraft and navigation.

Always carry waterproofs, spare sweater, map and compass,
whistle, first aid kit, emergency food and a polythene survival bag.
In winter you should have extra spare clothing and emergency food,

and a good torch. You might also like to split between the group a sleeping bag and a stove and pan although, if you are camping, you are likely to have these with you anyway.

Never undertake an expedition which is beyond your training, experience or fitness. Keep to well-known routes until you are proficient at navigation and route-finding. Check on the rescue facilities available in the area in which you intend to walk and be aware of the procedure to use in case of accidents.

It is inadvisable to go into the mountains alone unless you are very experienced. Whether you go alone, with a companion or with a group, it is a good idea to leave details of your route with someone responsible. If you do this, it is extremely important that you report your safe return, for otherwise a rescue team may be called out needlessly.

Check the *local* weather forecast before you set off and do not be afraid to alter your plans if the conditions worsen unexpectedly.

Disused mines and quarries in mountainous areas can be dangerous and are rarely checked for safety. It is in your own interests to stay well clear of such sites.

Never venture on to snow and ice unless you are familiar with basic winter techniques. Mastering the use of an ice axe and crampons should be regarded as a *minimum* level of ability. You should understand the cause and effect of cornices and avalanches, especially when walking in the Scottish Highlands where conditions can be severe from November to May.

In the event of an accident, carry out immediate first aid and get the casualty off the hill. If you cannot do this yourselves, erect a shelter for the casualty and the rest of the group, and use the International Mountain Distress Signal (see below). Other people may be nearby and in a position to help. If evacuation is impossible, find a telephone, dial 999 and ask for the Police, then ask for Mountain Rescue.

*The International Mountain Distress Signal* is six rapid signals (by whistle, torch, shouting, etc.) repeated at intervals of one minute. This should be repeated until you are located. The answer is three rapid signals repeated at intervals of one minute.

*Respect the land*
The designation 'National Park' does not confer any special rights of ownership or access on the land. When travelling through enclosed farmland or sensitive areas, keep to public rights of way and permitted footpaths. If in doubt about access, seek local advice. Avoid crossing firing ranges and, particularly when north of the border, remember the Scottish deer-stalking season (August/September).

If you do not wish to camp on an official camp site, make sure you have the permission of the landowner *before* you pitch your tent. If you dig a hole to make a latrine, replace the turf before moving on. Take care with fires and stoves. There should be nothing to indicate you have camped when you leave.

Take *all* your litter home. If you bury it, animals may dig it up. Empty tins and plastic bags are particularly dangerous to wildlife. Glass bottles are totally unnecessary in the first place.

*Conserve wildlife*
Disturb neither domestic nor wild animals, and leave flowers and plants for everyone to enjoy. In any case, it is now illegal to pick many wild flowers. There are agreed closed seasons for various nature reserves and some other areas, and you should take heed of the notices posted at such places regarding access.

Do not pollute mountain streams by dam-building, dish-washing or any other activity. Any form of pollution can seriously affect the ecology of such streams and their surroundings.

*Take nothing* but photographs.
*Leave nothing* but footprints.
*Disturb nothing* but the air around you.

*Consider other people*
*Never* throw stones or any other objects over the tops of crags or down slopes, even if you cannot see anyone below you; there may well be climbers or other walkers hidden from view. If you accidentally dislodge a stone, immediately warn anyone who may be below you, *shouting* the standard call 'Below!'

Many mountaineers leave tents or rucksacks while they go off on a rock climb. Do not remove apparently deserted equipment.

Many people live and work in the mountains. Have consideration for their way of life and their privacy.

Only lead walks and expeditions when you are competent to do so.

Most people go into the mountains to enjoy the peace and quiet of their surroundings. Do nothing that would impinge upon this enjoyment.

*Be weatherwise*
Even in summer, weather conditions can change with incredible speed. Do not hesitate to turn back if the weather deteriorates; only fools press on regardless. High winds and icing can be serious hazards, and low cloud or mist will substantially reduce the speed of most parties. Be careful in such conditions. Walk at a speed which allows you to see as much as possible of the ground ahead.

After heavy rain, the crossing of many mountain streams (even by stepping stones or low bridges) may be impossible. Rather than attempting unorthodox crossing methods, you should travel up or down the stream to a safe crossing point.

Both summer and winter weather extremes pose particular problems for mountain walkers. You should know both the symptoms and treatment of heat exhaustion and mountain hypothermia (exhaustion/exposure). You should also know how to avoid such problems.

Walking expeditions in high, craggy mountain areas may require specialist skills, including the use of ropes. Winter mountain-walking, especially in Scotland, can be a serious undertaking. Apart from the hazards posed by cornices and avalanches, darkness falls early and general conditions are usually far more extreme than elsewhere in Britain.

(Based upon *The Mountain Code* published by the British Mountaineering Council.)

**Appendix IV: Further reading**
If you visit any bookshop or library you will find that there is a
wealth of literature about outdoor activities and mountaineering.
Although this bibliography is far from comprehensive, I have tried
to give a representative coverage of the subjects available, and you
are almost certain to find something of interest.

Although some of the books listed are now out of print, they may
still be available from second-hand bookshops or public libraries.

GENERAL MOUNTAINCRAFT

*Avalanche Enigma*, Colin Fraser, John Murray, London, 1966.
*Avalanche and Snow Safety*, Colin Fraser, John Murray, London,
    1978.
*Backpackers' Manual, The*, Cameron McNeish, Oxford Illustrated
    Press, Yeovil, 1984.
*First Aid for Hillwalkers*, Jane Renouf and Stewart Hulse,
    Cicerone, Cumbria, 1982.
*Mountaincraft and Leadership*, Eric Langmuir, Scottish Sports
    Council/MLTB, Edinburgh, 1984.
*Mountaineering*, Alan Blackshaw, Penguin, London, 1970.
*Mountaineering: The Freedom of the Hills*, ed. E. Peters, The
    Mountaineers, Seattle, 1982.
*Mountaineering First Aid*, Lentz, Macdonald and Carline, The
    Mountaineers, Seattle, 1985.
*Mountain Hazards*, Kevin Walker, Constable, London, 1988.
*Mountain Navigation Techniques*, Kevin Walker, Constable,
    London, 1986.
*Mountain Weather for Climbers*, David Unwin, Cordee, Leicester,
    1978.
*Safety on Mountains*, British Mountaineering Council, Manchester,
    1975.
*Start Backpacking*, Mike Marriott, Stanley Paul, London, 1981.

## GENERAL INTEREST

*Annapurna*, Maurice Herzog, Jonathan Cape, London, 1952.

*Classic Walks*, Ken Wilson and Richard Gilbert, Diadem, London, 1982.

*Conquistadors of the Useless*, Lionel Terray, Gollancz (out of print).

*Everest the Hard Way*, Chris Bonington, Hodder & Stoughton, London, 1976.

*High Adventure*, Edmund Hillary, Hodder & Stoughton, London, 1955.

*I Chose to Climb*, Chris Bonington, Gollancz, London, 1969.

*Mountaincraft*, G. W. Young, Methuen, 1949.

*Mountaineering in Scotland/Undiscovered Scotland*, W. H. Murray, Diadem, London, 1979.

*Next Horizon*, Chris Bonington, Hodder & Stoughton, London, 1976.

*Nothing Venture, Nothing Win*, Edmund Hillary, Hodder & Stoughton, London, 1975.

*One Man's Mountains*, Tom Patey, Gollancz, London, 1971.

*Sacred Summits*, Peter Boardman, Hodder & Stoughton, London, 1982.

*South Col*, Wilfred Noyce, Heinemann, London, 1954.

*The Ascent of Everest*, J. Hunt, Hodder & Stoughton, London, 1953.

*The Games Climbers Play*, ed. Ken Wilson, Diadem, London, 1978.

*The Shining Mountain*, Peter Boardman, Hodder & Stoughton, London, 1987.

*The Winding Trail*, ed. Roger Smith, Diadem, London, 1981.

*Wild Walks*, Richard Gilbert and Ken Wilson, Diadem, London, 1988.

## MAGAZINES

*The Great Outdoors*, *Climber*, *Footloose*, *Mountain*, *High* (Journal of the BMC), *Outdoor Action*, *Pursuit*, *Wilderness Odyssey*, etc.

Many of these magazines carry stories, instructional articles, gear tests and surveys, as well as news and gossip. There are also directories of equipment retailers and clubs, and the magazines are excellent sources of information.

## GUIDEBOOKS

Most mountain areas in Britain are covered by walking and climbing guidebooks. In addition to those published and distributed by major companies such as Constable, there are several small concerns (e.g. Heritage Guides) who produce guidebooks of both a specialist and general nature.

### Appendix V: Useful organizations and addresses

With the increasing growth in popularity of mountain activities, there is almost certain to be a mountaineering or walking club in your area, no matter where you live. Details of these can usually be found in the back of the relevant magazines, or you can write to the representative body:

BRITISH MOUNTAINEERING COUNCIL,
Crawford House
Precinct Centre
Booth Street East
Manchester M13 9RZ
Tel.  061-273 5835 (general enquiries and membership)
       061-273 5839 (publications, courses, etc.)
       061-272 5163 (insurance, reciprocal rights card)

Details of Scottish clubs can be obtained from the secretary of the MOUNTAINEERING COUNCIL OF SCOTLAND. Their current address can be obtained either from the BMC or from:

SCOTTISH SPORTS COUNCIL
1 St Colme Street
Edinburgh EH3 6AA
Tel. 031-225 8411

If you are interested in general walking, you might like to contact:

THE RAMBLERS' ASSOCIATION
1–5 Wandsworth Road
London SW8 2LJ
Tel. 01-582 6826

If you are interested in general backpacking, you might like to contact:

THE BACKPACKERS' CLUB
20 St Michaels Road
Tilehurst
Reading RG3 4RP

Courses in various aspects of mountaincraft are run at the Sports Council's National Centres:

Plas-y-Brenin
Capel Curig
Nr Betws-y-Coed
Gwynedd LL24 OET
Tel. 06904 280 (bookings)
     06904 214 or 363 (offices)

or

Plas-menai
Llanfairisgaer
Caernarfon
Gwynedd
Tel. 0248 670964

or

Glenmore Lodge
Aviemore
Inverness-shire PH22 1QU
Tel.  047-986 276 (bookings)
      047-986 256 (offices)

In addition, the BMC runs a variety of training courses, and there
are many other excellent organizations which offer holidays and
courses to individuals and groups. Their addresses can be found in
relevant magazines. The author offers courses in various aspects of
mountaincraft, full details of which are available from:

KEVIN WALKER MOUNTAIN ACTIVITIES
James Street
Llangynidr
Crickhowell
Powys NP8 1NN
Tel.  0874 730554

Information about the Association of British Mountain Guides can
be obtained from their secretary, Alan Hunt, at:

11 Dean Park Crescent
Edinburgh
Tel.  031-332 3468

Information on the National Parks can be obtained from the
Information Officer at the relevant address.

BRECON BEACONS NATIONAL PARK
7 Glamorgan Street
Brecon
Powys LD3 7DP
Tel.  0874 4437

## DARTMOOR NATIONAL PARK
Parke
Haytor Road
Bovey Tracey
Newton Abbot
Devon TQ13 9JQ
Tel. 0626 832093

## EXMOOR NATIONAL PARK
Exmoor House
Dulverton
Somerset
Tel. 0398 23665

## LAKE DISTRICT NATIONAL PARK
Brockhole
Windermere
Cumbria LA23 1LJ
Tel. 09662 3467

## NORTHUMBERLAND NATIONAL PARK
Eastburn
South Park
Hexham
Northumberland NE46 1BS
Tel. 0434 605555

## NORTH YORK MOORS NATIONAL PARK
The Old Vicarage
Bondgate
Helmsley
North Yorkshire YO6 5BP
Tel. 04392 657

**PEAK DISTRICT NATIONAL PARK**
Losehill Hall
Castleton
Derbyshire S30 2WB
Tel.  0433 20373

**PEMBROKESHIRE COAST NATIONAL PARK**
County Offices
Haverfordwest
Dyfed SA61 1QZ
Tel.  0437 4591

**SNOWDONIA NATIONAL PARK**
Penrhyndeudraeth
Gwynedd LL48 6LS
Tel.  0766 770274

**YORKSHIRE DALES NATIONAL PARK**
Colvend
Hebden Road
Grassington
Skipton
North Yorkshire BD23 5LB
Tel.  0756 752748

# Index

Figures in *italics* refer to illustrations or diagrams